The Rise and Fall of Black Wall Street

AND

The Seven Key Empowerment Principles

The Rise and Fall of Black Wall Street

AND

The Seven Key Empowerment Principles

BY

Robin Walker

REKLAW EDUCATION LTD
London (U.K.)

CONTENTS

OPENING REMARKS

About Part One

The Rise and Fall of Black Wall Street details the inspiring story of a brilliant Black business district in Tulsa, Oklahoma. African Americans created an economic miracle in Tulsa in the 1910s that ultimately resulted in the creation of perhaps 600 businesses. They also created a hospital, libraries, public schools and at least one megachurch.

These entrepreneurial African Americans owned theatres, hotels, restaurants, rented accommodation, clothing firms, printing firms, newspapers and transportation companies. Also present were the educated professionals who also made a great contribution. At the weekends Black Tulsa came alive as the Black owned bars, night clubs and the illegal establishments throbbed to the sounds of Blues and Jazz.

Many Black Tulsans created great fortunes. A few became millionaires, some owning private planes. Many Black homes contained china, fine linens, beautiful furniture, and grand pianos. An organiser of the National Negro Business League described the business district as "a regular Monte Carlo."

However, ruin struck long ago. Nearby Whites, jealous of the successes of Black Tulsans, unleashed an orgy of violence against the Black Business District. With high-placed backing and support, the conquerors launched an efficiently destructive race war. This is what caused the Fall of Black Wall Street.

In recounting this story, I draw from the findings of earlier scholars whose research I am indebted to: Alfred L. Brophy, Scott Ellsworth, R. Halliburton, Hannibal B. Johnson and Lee E. Williams. I, however, take full responsibility for any errors that may unintentionally have crept into this work.

About Part Two

What does it take for an individual to replicate the kind of economic success that the people of Black Wall $treet achieved? In the second part of this book, I present my own ideas on what I believe it takes to become successful. I outline *The Seven Key Empowerment Principles* that any individual needs to use as a minimum to replicate that kind of success.

Following in the footsteps of George Subira and believing that poverty is the biggest problem that Black Communities need to solve, I show that individuals need five things to make it in the money game.

They need Inspiration, Correct Knowledge, a Money Management System, a Personal Plan, and the Seven Key Empowerment Principles.

Inspiration gives individuals 'the WHY.' Correct Knowledge gives individuals 'the TARGET.' A Money Management System and the Personal Plan gives individuals 'the HOW.' Finally, The Seven Key Empowerment Principles gives 'the CEMENT' that holds 'the WHY,' 'the HOW' and 'the TARGET' together.

About Part Three

In the third part of this book, I introduce the lectures, courses and other products that I deliver on Black Economic Empowerment. I also give details of how to contact me.

Read and enjoy!

Robin Walker 2016

PART ONE

THE RISE AND FALL OF BLACK WALL STREET

INTRODUCTION: OPPORTUNITIES IN THE PROMISED LAND

In 1900 there were 27 all-Black towns in the region now called Oklahoma. Not all writers agree with this figure. One writer put the numbers of all-Black towns in the region as over 60. Which ever be the case, many of these Black Oklahomans eventually relocated to the 'promised land' of Tulsa. The concept of the 'promised land' was coined by a Black man, John Williams, and then immortalised by Dr Scott Ellsworth in his masterly book *Death in a Promised Land,* 1982.

There was much oil wealth in the area. This proved to be a magnet that attracted people. It also led other industries to boom indirectly from the oil wealth.

One inspiring story was that of John Williams, mentioned earlier. He was originally a worker in the Thompson Ice Cream Company. The job paid well enough--he was the first Black person in the area to be able to afford a car. However, he quit his job to open his first business: the East End Garage on Greenwood Avenue.

Figure 1. 1912 photograph of John, Loula, and Bill Williams in a state-of-the-art 1911 Norwalk car.

Figure 2. Page from *Booker T. Washington High School: Tulsa, Oklahoma,* (June 1921 Year Book) showing the Williams family and their businesses. The business captions from left to right are as follows: Williams Confectionary, East End Garage and Williams Dreamland Theater.

Figure 3. The Williams Dreamland Theatre and Boarding House.

By 1912 he owned an impressive three-storey brick building on 101 North Greenwood. On the ground floor was a confectionery owned by his wife, Loula Williams. It possessed a 12 foot fountain and seating for nearly 50 patrons selling candy, ice cream and soda. It was Black Tulsa's first commercial refreshment place, excluding the other establishments which sold illicit whisky. On the first floor was the living space of the Williams family. On the second floor was office space they rented out to dentists, doctors and lawyers.

In 1914 the Williams family built a second building on Greenwood Avenue. With equipment bought from a bankrupt theatre in Oklahoma City, the ground floor became the Williams Dreamland Theatre which featured theatrical reviews, live musicals and silent movies accompanied by a pianist. One source claims that the theatre had seating for 700 patrons. The first floor was a 21 room boarding house (i.e. rented accommodation).

Mrs Loula Williams was described as 'perhaps the best business women of the race in Oklahoma' by *The Black Dispatch,* a Black Oklahoma newspaper. She also owned a theatre in the town of Muskogee and another in Okmulgee.

This wealth and opulence was shared by many Black Tulsans: Simon Berry, O. W. Gurley, Mabel Little and J. B. Stradford. This lecture essay aims to tell some of their stories and paint a picture of what Black business people can achieve through their own efforts.

CHAPTER ONE: THE EVOLUTION OF BLACK TULSA (1834 TO 1921)

The Early History

African Americans migrated to Oklahoma from Arkansas, Louisiana, Mississippi and Texas, looking to improve their lives. Others were brought there as enslaved captives by various Native American nations during the 'Trail of Tears' of 1831 to 1838; the United States government removed the Cherokee, Chickasaw, Choctaw, Creek and Seminole Nations from their lands to what would become the State of Oklahoma. One writer suggests that one third of the people who travelled with the Indian Nations were Black.

It may surprise readers to know that some Native American nations also had Africans in bondage. It is, however, possible that enslavement by Native Americans was significantly different to enslavement by Europeans.

The Creek Indians founded 'Tallasi' sometime after 1834. The first Blacks there were their captives. Tallasi is the settlement that would evolve into 'Tulsey Town' and ultimately 'Tulsa'.

After the American Civil War and the emancipation that followed, the Black freedmen remained in the area. Freedmen in the Coweta District of the Creek Nation, where Tulsa was located, were occasionally chosen for public positions.

In the late nineteenth century 'Tallasi' became better known as 'Tulsey Town.' Boosting the Black population were an influx of people from Missouri, Mississippi and Georgia. The Blacks founded the Vernon AME Church in 1895 and the Macedonia Baptist Church in 1897.

Why did these other Blacks come to this region? Ralph Ellison said that: 'many of the descendents of freed slaves ... considered it a territory of hope, and a place where they could create their own opportunities ... [F]or Negroes it had a traditional association with freedom which had entered their folklore.' Moreover, Oklahoma 'lacked the intensities of custom, tradition and manners which 'colored' the institutions of the Old South.'

Many Blacks did find a better life in Oklahoma. In all-Black towns such as Boley, Red Bird, Rentiesville, Taft and Tullahassee, African Americans became successful business entrepreneurs and directed their own community affairs. Some of these people would also relocate to Tulsa.

Figures 4 and 5. Tulsa in 1900 showing the main street and oil extraction industry to the south of the city. Petroleum was first discovered near Bartlesville, Indian Territory in 1897, fifty miles north of Tulsa. In 1901 petroleum was discovered near Beaumont, Texas, and at Red Fork, Indian Territory.

Beginnings of the Tulsa Economic Miracle

Some writers present Mr O. W. Gurley, a wealthy Black landowner from Arkansas, as the founder of Black Tulsa. He purchased 40 acres of land on moving to Tulsa at the end of the nineteenth century, and stipulated that it was 'only to be sold to Colored [i.e. Blacks]'.

Among Gurley's first businesses was a rooming house. It was located on a dusty trail near the rail tracks. By 1906, this road was given the name 'Greenwood Avenue', named for a city in Mississippi. However, one important source document, the *Booker T. Washington High School: Tulsa, Oklahoma,* (June 1921 Year Book), consistently calls this road 'Greenwood Street'. Which ever be the case, the area became popular among African American migrants fleeing oppression in Mississippi. They found refuge in Gurley's building, as the racial persecution typical of the south was not present in this area. In addition to his rooming house, Gurley built three two-story buildings and five residences. Moreover, he bought an 80-acre farm in Rogers County. Gurley also founded the Vernon AME Church. One writer dates this building to 1895.

Many consider the evolution of Tulsa to be the story of two segregated cities rather than one united city. The White residents began calling the area north of the Frisco rail tracks 'Little Africa'. Later centred on Greenwood Avenue (or Street), this boulevard was important since it ran north for over a mile from the Frisco Railroad yards, and it was one of the few streets that did not pass through both Black and White areas. The Black inhabitants of Greenwood took pride in this area because it was something they had control of themselves and did not have to share with White Tulsa. The Acme Brick Company was based two blocks north of Greenwood. This company made the bricks for the Greenwood area.

Another distinguished pioneer, Mr J. B. Stradford (given as 'Stafford' by some writers), arrived in Tulsa in 1899. He felt that Black people had a better chance of economic progress if they amassed their resources, worked in concert and supported each other's enterprises. To this end, he bought large tracts of real estate in northeastern Tulsa, which he subdivided and sold exclusively to other African Americans.

Incidentally, Stradford went on to built the Stradford Hotel on 301 North Greenwood, telephone number Osage 4238, where Blacks could enjoy the amenities of the downtown hotels that served only Whites. It had 68 modern rooms, a dining room and a cafe. This hotel quickly gained a reputation as the largest Black-owned hotel in the United States at the time. In the same property, Stradford owned a Real Estate, Loan and Investment company, telephone number 3386. Moreover, A. L. Ferguson owned a business in the property, telephone Osage 9312. The advertising claims it was: 'THE COOLEST ICE CREAM PARLOR IN TULSA'. Moreover, the business sold medicines, cigars, tobacco, toiletries and medical prescriptions.

In 1900 the population of Tulsa was estimated at 1,390 people where Blacks made up 5% of the population. Most of the Blacks were day labourers, servants and housewives. However, even at this early date, there was a Black lawyer, a blacksmith, a stonemason, and a full-time preacher.

In 1906 a Black newspaper was established called the Tulsa *Guide* edited by a certain G. W. Hutchins. He also was an attorney.

However, in 1907 Oklahoma officially became an American state. The White power structure immediately enforced a series of laws to turn Oklahoma into a White dominated state. They aimed to de-power the

Blacks and the 'Indians.' The key issue seemed to be control over the oil boom across Oklahoma. The White power structure did not want this oil boom being controlled by Blacks or Native Americans. By 1907, however, Black Tulsa had 2 doctors, 1 barbershop and 3 grocers.

The importance of the oil industry cannot be emphasized enough. By 1907 Oklahoma was the leading state in the United States in terms of oil production. At one time the boom town of Tulsa itself contained offices for 126 oil companies. By 1913 Oklahoma produced one quarter of all the oil in the United States. Production in 1915 reached 300,000 barrels of oil on a daily basis.

By 1910 Tulsa grew to a population of 18,182 people with Blacks comprising 10% of the population. This same year saw the birth of the first Black trade union, The Hod Carriers Local No. 199, designed to protect the interests of brick layers, plasterers and masons. In 1911 Barney Cleaver became the first Black police officer in Tulsa.

Greenwood Avenue (or Street) evolved into a commercial district of red brick buildings. With the implementation of segregation, the Greenwood boundaries of separateness which defined Black Tulsa, and exists today, were established: Pine Street to the North, Lansing Street to the East, Archer Street and the Frisco tracks to the South, and Cincinnati Street to the West. Another important landmark in Black Tulsa was Detroit Avenue, along the edge of Standpipe Hill, which contained the wealthier houses of the business owners, doctors and lawyers. Finally, outside of the commercial district, a lot of Black people owned farmland. Many of these landowners went into the oil business.

To give an example of the staggering amount of money generated by oil rich African Americans in Oklahoma, *The Tulsa Star* of 7 February 1914 carried an article called: *WHITE MEN WOULD WED RICH COLORED GIRL*. The article tells of a Black girl from the all Black town of Taft, Oklahoma '14 or 15 years old, whose income from her oil wells is something like $15,000.00 a month. Her name is Sarah Rector.' The article further says, with almost British understatement: 'Her wealth, however, is not much out of the ordinary for the dark skinned lads and lasses over in that part of the state.' Once we recognise (i) that $15,000 per month in 1914 dwarfs $15,000 today, and (ii) Sarah Rector was ONE OF MANY oil rich Black youngsters, this information is a cause for deep and profound reflection.

It is instructive to find out why so many Black people came to Tulsa during these early years.

Figure 6. Funeral Car of Jackson Undertaking Company, 1921. Probably the same Sam Jackson mentioned by Mabel Little, see below.

Mabel Little was a 17 year old who arrived in Tulsa in 1913 from the all-Black town of Boley, Oklahoma. Her opinions of the district were as follows:

> Black businesses flourished. I remember Huff's Café on Cincinnati and Archer it was a thriving meeting place in the [B]lack community. You could go there almost any time, and just about everybody who was anybody would be there or on their way. There were also two popular barbecue spots, Tipton's and Uncle Steve's. J. D. Mann had a grocery store. His wife was a music teacher. We had two funeral parlors, owned by morticians Sam Jackson and Hardel Ragston. Down on what went by the name of 'Deep Greenwood' was a clique of eateries, a panorama of lively dance halls, barber shops and theatres glittering in the nightlight, and a number of medical and dental offices.

Mable Little came to Tulsa with $1.50 in her pocket. From cleaning motel rooms, she saved her money and ultimately went into business. She owned the Little Rose Beauty Salon on 615 East Indiana Avenue, telephone number 1895. Her business specialised in hair dressing using the 'Taylor System'. Manicuring and facial massage was also on offer. She also bought rental property and, together with her husband, owned a restaurant next door to her salon.

By 1913 a part of Greenwood Avenue was now being called 'Deep Greenwood.' It was also called the 'Negro Wall Street.' The White community called it 'Little Africa.' An organiser of the National Negro Business League, the organisation founded by the great Booker T. Washington, called it "a regular Monte Carlo." There was another Black newspaper at this time called *Weekly Planet.* Professor J. H. Hill edited this newspaper. Ed Goodwin grew up in Tulsa where his father built a grocery business in 1915. He remembered that the city was "once a Mecca for the Negro businessman--a showplace."

Mary Parrish left Rochester, New York, to come to Tulsa in 1918. Eventually she ran a school on 103 ½ North Greenwood Street, telephone numbers Osage 2157 and 3339. Her school taught typewriting and shorthand. She gave her reasons for coming to Tulsa as follows:

> I had heard of this town since girlhood and of the many opportunities here to make money. But I came not to Tulsa as many came, lured by the dream of making money and better myself in the financial world, but because of the wonderful co-operation I observed among our people, and especially the harmony of spirit and action that existed between the businessmen and women … On Greenwood one could find a variety of business places which would be a credit to any section of the town. In the residential section there were homes of beauty and splendor which would please the most critical eye. The schools and many churches were well attended.

Professor Alfred Brophy author of *Reconstructing the Dreamland,* believes he has detected other reasons why Blacks came to Tulsa:

> Greenwood's residents spoke about the need to prevent lynchings, to protect voting rights, to develop the community. Central to their thinking was the idea of the rule of law: that the government should establish impartial rules and apply them equally to [W]hites and [B]lacks ... Blacks--even if segregated-- should receive the same treatment as [W]hites on railroads; [B]lack schools should be equal in funding and quality to [W]hite schools; [B]lacks should be allowed to register to vote and serve on juries on the same terms as [W]hites; police officers should treat [B]lacks with the same respect they accorded [W]hites. Those ideals about law were promulgated in the pages of the [B]lack newspapers. Sometimes they appeared in more formal arenas, like federal courts, where [B]lacks filed suits to protect their right to equal treatment. They won two cases in the United States Supreme Court in the 1910s. One struck down Oklahoma's grandfather clause; the other, Oklahoma's railroad segregation statute, which allowed railroads to provide unequal treatment to [B]lacks.

Black Tulsa began to flourish. According to local historian, Henry

Whitlow, White racism was a major impetus for the growth of the Black Business District. Blacks could work in the White areas as common labourers, domestics and in the service sector, but their money was not welcomed by the White businesses. In fact, segregation in Tulsa was more complete than in other American cities. Consequently the Black community had to create their own businesses in order to be able to spend their money. Illustrating this idea, Pasha O, in an internet essay, says: 'The dollar circulated 36 to 100 times, sometimes taking a year for currency to leave the community. Now a dollar leaves the Black community in 15 minutes.'

According to other writers, another impetus that moved Greenwood forward was the presence of Black Veterans returning to Tulsa after the end of World War I in 1918. These Veterans were asked to fight to defend US freedom abroad and these ideas must have permeated through Black Tulsan society on their return. These men believed that they had earned full citizenship, partnership and acceptance.

As an example of this, Professor Brophy cites a 1918 speech given by Roscoe Dunjee, editor of Oklahoma City's Black newspaper, *The Black Dispatch*, where he said:

> President Wilson [the then US president] says we go out to make the world safe for democracy ... Democracy ... means that [B]lack men as well as [W]hite men shall sit in jury boxes and everywhere. Democracy means, if we would breathe the 'pure air' of which Wilson speaks, that spoliation and exploitation of [B]lack men's property shall cease, it means that segregation, Jim Crowism and mob violence must die, and that in its stead there must rise justice, equity and fairness.

Education, Newspapers, etcetera

By 1921, the Black population now numbered 11,000 people out of a total of 98,874. They had a Black public library. They had 2 Black public schools, i.e. the Paul Laurence Dunbar and the Booker T. Washington. Three quarters of Black children of school age were now in school. Tulsa had the second lowest Black illiteracy rate of any county in Oklahoma.

The curriculum at the Booker T. Washington School was as follows: The youngest pupils, the FRESHMAN CLASS, studied Latin, English, algebra, drawing, domestic science and art, manual training, ancient history and vocal music. The year above, the SOPHOMORE CLASS studied Latin, English, geometry, domestic art, drawing, medieval and modern history,

Figure 7. The Booker T. Washington School, Tulsa, 1921.

economics, music, domestic science and manual training. The JUNIOR CLASS studied English, algebra, commercial arithmetic, drawing, manual training, business spelling, chemistry, English history, civics, domestic art, domestic science and vocal music. Finally, the SENIOR CLASS studied English, physics, geometry solid, typewriting, vocal music, domestic science, manual training, American history, psychology, trigonometry plane, bookkeeping, drawing, domestic art and shorthand. In addition, all classes were required to take part in some form of athletics.

Black Tulsa had 13 churches. One had an attendance of 950 people and cost $135,000 to build and furnish. There was a Black hospital. There were 3 fraternal lodges, i.e. the Masons, the Knights of Pythias and the Independent Order of Odd Fellows. Finally, there were 2 Black newspapers, i.e. *The Tulsa Star* and the Oklahoma *Sun*.

Mr Andrew J. Smitherman owned *The Tulsa Star*. He previously worked with W. H. Twine on the *Muskogee Cimiter*, a Black newspaper based in Muskogee, Oklahoma. After this, he started his own paper, the *Muskogee Star*, in 1912. In the following year, he moved the *Star* to Tulsa where it was based on 501 North Greenwood Street. Smitherman is said to have practiced law, like Twine, in addition to operating his newspaper.

Smitherman used *The Tulsa Star* as a mouthpiece to popularise his staunch Democratic ideals to Black subscribers in an era when the Republicans were more popular amongst African Americans. He preached

Figure 8. *The Tulsa Star*, 27 November 1920.

self-reliance and militant action to protect Blacks against the tide of KKK inspired racial violence occurring around the country. Smitherman consistently lectured the community on why they needed to arm and protect themselves from lynchings. Later on, Smitherman rushed to the scene of the Tulsa race war to provide assistance, and not just to report on it.

The Tulsa Star supported Black businesses with adverts dotted throughout. It also had a page entitled *Tulsa's Colored Business Directory.* In the paper were adverts from bakers, barbers, cobblers, hotels, etcetera, but also Black owned attorneys, baggage men, blacksmiths, chiropractors, contractors and builders, dentists, employment agencies, furniture stores, insurance, newspaper distributors, oil investment opportunities, photographic studios, plumbers, tax specialists, taxis and used piano dealerships.

Incidentally, Smitherman also owned the North Elgin Grocery and Confectionary on 404 North Elgin, telephone number 4881. The business sold: 'Staple and Fancy Groceries, Fresh Meats, Milk, Cigars, Tobaccos, Cold Drinks, Nuts and Fancy Candies'.

Little Africa at the Height of its Prosperity

Black Tulsa had 1 shop selling 'feed and grain', 1 undertaker with caskets ranging from $50 to $1000 with a $10,000 limousine to transport the bereaved family members, 2 garages/filling stations, 6 estate agents/loan companies/insurance companies, 5 builders/contractors, 2 dressmakers, 4 shoemakers/repairs with up-to-date machinery, 10 tailors, 1 printer with $25,000 worth of equipment, 12 barbers, 3 hairdressers/beauty salons, 5 cleaners/hatters/dyers, a number of plumbers, 1 upholsterer, 2 photographers, 1 jeweller and 15 physicians, dentists and surgeons. It must again be emphasized that many of these medical practitioners had invested heavily in up-to-date apparatus and equipment.

Greenwood Avenue (or Street) was the 'Negro Wall Street' as also was a portion of Archer Street. This area had two and three-storey red brick buildings including a dry goods store (Black Tulsa had 2 in total), groceries and meat markets (Black Tulsa had 41 in total), confectioneries (Black Tulsa had 4 in total), restaurants (Black Tulsa had 30 in total), billiard halls (Black Tulsa had 9 in total), 11 boarding houses (i.e. rented accommodation), 4 hotels (Black Tulsa had 5 in total), 2 Black theatres--of which one, according to one source, had 700 seats, in addition there were doctors, lawyers and professionals.

The *Booker T. Washington High School: Tulsa, Oklahoma,* (June 1921 Year Book), has adverts from local businesses. This valuable information allows us to reconstruct where SOME of the businesses were as we walk down Greenwood, Archer and Cincinnati streets at the height of their prosperity.

J. T. Taylor and J. L. Duncan owned the Union Grocery on Greenwood Street. Their advertising emphasises quality, price and excellent customer service: 'WE SOLICIT YOUR PATRONAGE STRICTLY ON OUR SERVICE, QUALITY, AND PRICE. WE THANK THE PUBLIC FOR HELPING US TO BUILD UP OUR BUSINESS TO ITS PRESENT STANDING, AND WITH YOUR FUTURE PATRONAGE WE INTEND TO GIVE THE BEST IN QUALITY, SERVING YOU WITH UNLIMITED COURTESY AT THE LOWEST PRICE FOR QUALITY.'

The Earl Real Estate Company was on 101 North Greenwood Street, telephone number Osage 6673. The telephone number indicates that this business could afford a telephone at this early period. By contrast, many homes in the UK did NOT have telephones as late as 1980! The Estate Company specialised in farm lands, city property and oil leases.

H. L. Byars ran a Merchant Tailor business on 105 North Greenwood, telephone number Osage 3043. Their advertising suggests that they handled: 'CLEANING, PRESSING, REPAIRING, EXPERT ALTERATION--HAND MADE PANTS [i.e. trousers] A SPECIALITY'. Also: 'HATS [were] CLEANED AND BLOCKED'. Attentive to customer service: 'WORK [was] CALLED FOR AND DELIVERED'.

Mr O. W. Gurley, one of the two pioneers of Little Africa, owned the Gurley Hotel at 112 North Greenwood, the street's first commercial enterprise, valued at $55,000. Also in the complex was the Dock Eastmand & Hughes Cafe. Also there was the The Brunswick Smoke House and Billiards Parlor owned by W. M. Shore. This business specialised in 'CONFECTIONS, SOFT DRINKS, CIGARS, TOBACCO, FANCY FRUITS AND CANDIES.'

Mr Anderson owned Y. M. C. A. Tailors on 114 North Greenwood Street. Their advertising says: 'CLEANING, PRESSING, REPAIRING AND EXPERT ALTERATIONS AT ALL TIMES'. It also says: 'WE CLEAN AND REPAIR CLOTHES OF ALL MATERIAL[,] WORK GUARANTEED'. Moreover: 'Our Stock of Spring and Summer Goods is Heavy [sic], so Come in and Pay us a Visit. WE CALL AND DELIVER'.

O. W. Gurley, mentioned above, also owned a two-story building at 119 North Greenwood. It housed Carter's Barbershop, Hardy Rooms, a pool

Figure 9. Advertisement for the Satisfactory Tailoring Company, 418 E. Archer Street, Tulsa, 1921.

hall, and a cigar store. Also there was Newkirk Wholesale and Retail Confections owned by A. S. Newkirk, telephone number 6675. Describing the business as 'Dealers in Novelties' and a place where 'Photos of Quality Made Day and Night', Newkirk also offered 'Penants [sic]' as a 'Speciality'. Pennants are tapered flags.

The Nails Bros. Shoe Market was on 121 North Greenwood, telephone number Osage 163. The advert for this business says: 'I REPAIR ANY STYLE SHOE MADE TO ORDER, SPECIAL WORK DONE WHILE YOU WAIT'. It also says: 'WE CALL FOR AND DELIVER'.

An individual called Stokenberry managed the Palace Shining Parlor on 122 North Greenwood. This business had the motto: 'Prompt, Accurate and Generous Service'.

Elliott & Hooker was on 124 North Greenwood, telephone number Osage 7682. Their specialities were in 'Clothing, Shoes,' and 'Ladies' Ready-to-wear.'

W. M. Kyle owned the Red Wing Drug Store on 202 North Greenwood, telephone number Osage 4016. Their advertising explains that: 'The Red Wing Drug Store's principal and policy is accuracy, Purity and Service, and upon these principals we challenge all for Superiority. We have in our prescription department the greatest variety of chemicals, making it possible to fill from the simplest to the most technical and complicated prescription, always under the supervision of three Registered Pharmacists. We welcome you for inspection of our entire stock and to make our Drug Store your headquarters for health, business and pleasure.' Moreover: 'OUR STORES OFFER THE YOUNG MEN AND WOMEN OF OUR SCHOOLS AN EXAMPLE OF RACE ACCOMPLISHMENT--THE BEST SERVICE OF ANY SIMILAR ESTABLISHMENT AND THE BEST MERCHANDISE TO BE HAD FOR THE MONEY. TRY US BEFORE GOING ELSEWHERE!!!'

Mrs M. N. Hardy owned a Madam C. J. Walker Beauty Parlor on 210 North Greenwood Street. The business offered a scientific scalp treatment, hair treatment and specialist facial treatment. Their advertising cryptically says: 'There is a spirit of recognition which holds a lofty position in every woman who pays compliment to the truth whenever found.' We also read: 'For General Massage, Pimples, Blackheads, Eczema, or any skin disease. Manicuring, Shampoos, Marcel Waving, and all kinds of electric treatment for scalp and body massages, OUR WORK GUARANTEED'. Also at this same address, C. L. Netherland owned the New State Barber Shop. Managed by J. A. Anderson, the business had the motto: 'Generosity & Service'.

The Satisfactory Tailoring Company (figure 9) was on 418 East Archer Street, telephone number Osage 3771. Their advert says: 'FOR PERFECT FITTING MADE TO MEASURE, CLOTHING, GUARANTEED CLEANING AND PRESSING[,] DYEING, ALTERING AND REPAIRING'. They also promised: 'MOTOR DELIVERY TO ALL PARTS OF THE CITY'.

J. L. Grier owned the Grier Shoe Shop on 518 East Archer Street at the corner with Greenwood, telephone number Osage 7953. Specialising in ladies shoes, Grier claims: 'TRY US ONCE AND YOU WILL TRY US TWICE.'

Mme Dora Wells owned the Wells Garment Factory on 613 East Archer Street, telephone number Osage 2365. This factory had a 'Speciality in Ladies Clothing.'

The Jackson Undertaking Company mentioned earlier (figure 6) was on

Figure 10. Detail from *Booker T. Washington High School: Tulsa, Oklahoma,* (June 1921 Year Book) showing the Grier Shoe Shop business card.

622 East Archer, telephone number 4710. Its motto was particularly simple. It was just one word: 'SERVICE'.

Cavers French Dry Cleaning Hatters and Tailors were on 4 North Cincinnati, telephone number Osage 3152. Their advertising positions them as the 'headquarters for ladies fine garments both dry and wet cleaning'. In addition, they made a 'Speciality of Ladies' Evening Gowns, Party Dresses, Kid Gloves and Fur Sets. We Clean, Bleach and Block Hats. We have a Complete Outfit of Sanitary Dry Cleaning Machinery. A Modern Plant. Suits Made to Order--500 Samples to select from. All Work Guaranteed--Our Dust Proof Auto will call for and deliver to all parts of the city.'

Carl Whitaker managed the Frisco Shining Parlor on 8 North Cincinnati, telephone number Osage 659. With dyeing as their speciality, their advertising says: 'ANY Kind of LEATHER CLEANED'. Also 'SWADE [sic] SHOES A SPECIALITY'. Finally, we are told that 'Hand Bags [were] Cleaned and Dyed.'

Brown's Cafe was located on 12 North Cincinnati Avenue, telephone number Osage 5880, it was open 24 hours each day. Their advertising describes it as: 'THE PLACE WHERE [the] HIGH COST OF LIVING HAS TAKEN A FALL'. Moreover: 'QUALITY, QUANTITY, AND COURTEOUS TREATMENT IS OUR WAY TO PLEASE--GIVE US A TRIAL'.

Mr and Mrs Cornelius Hunter owned the Liberty Cafe on 16 North Cincinnati Avenue. It was apparently: 'THE BEST PLACE IN TOWN TO EAT--OPEN DAY AND NIGHT'.

Finally, P. S. Thompson had a business called The Druggist [i.e. pharmacist]. It was on 23 North Cincinnati, telephone 4393.

On the side streets of Greenwood, Archer and Cincinnati were the illegal and semi-legal businesses. There were the 'Choc' joints (i.e. drinking houses selling 'Choctaw' beer, a drink supposedly associated with the Choctaw, a Native American nation). Also there were nightclubs, brothels, gambling parlours, and speakeasies. There were institutions selling illicit whiskey. People also had access to opium. There were gangsters and hoodlums. Also some of the poor Blacks lived in the side streets in shanties. Interestingly, many other poor Blacks lived in White areas in quarters located on their employer's lots. In total, one source states that 600 businesses flourished in Black Tulsa (legal and illegal). Black Tulsa came alive from Thursday evening through the weekend as Blacks from the White areas came to Black Tulsa to party. Blues and Jazz were the musical forms that accompanied Tulsan nightlife.

There were individual examples that illustrated the concept of *livin' phat*. At least 3 Blacks had fortunes of $1 million each. One source goes further and claims six Blacks had such large fortunes--some with private planes. Several Blacks had fortunes of $25,000 to $500,000. It must be remembered that $25,000 in 1921 dwarfs $25,000 today.

It became fashionable to dangle $20 gold pieces (watches) from a chain. One Black shoeshiner, Joe Heaton, reputedly owned 3 such gold pieces.

Simon Berry operated a bus, taxi and garage service that was turning over $500 per day. He owned his own plane. He also owned the Royal Hotel in Greenwood district. By the mid 1920s, Berry and another Black businessman (James Lee Northington) operated a popular airline charter service in Tulsa. He reinvested into the community and purchased land to establish a park for local residents to enjoy. Included in this park was a dance hall, picnic area and swimming pool.

Getting Some Opinions

As one web site put it: 'Tulsa's progressive African American community boasted some of the city's most elegant brick homes, well furnished with china, fine linens, beautiful furniture, and grand pianos.'

The Young Turks said: 'The best description of Black Wall Street, or Little Africa as it was also known, would be to compare it to a mini Beverly

Hills. It was the golden door of the Black community during 1900s, and it proved that African Americans could create a successful infrastructure.'

G. A. Gregg, an important official in the Y. M. C. A., remembered that: 'The Tulsa [C]olored people in every sense of the word were building a modern, up-to-date business city.'

Dr W. E. B. DuBois, the great African American social scientist said: "I have never seen a [C]olored community so highly organized as that of Tulsa ... The [C]olored people of Tulsa have accumulated property, have established stores and business organizations and have made money in oil."

Hitting Home the Point

It is interesting to compare the achievements of 11,000 Black Tulsans with 2 million Black Britons.

Where is the Black owned public library amongst Black Britons? What about the Black owned hospital? 11,000 Black Tulsans created 2 public schools: How many such schools have 2 million Black Britons created? What about the bus and taxi services, garages, oil wells, estate agents, insurance companies, restaurants, theatres, and hotels?

11,000 Black Tulsans had three, some say six, millionaires, some owning their own planes. It, again, must be remembered that $1 million in 1921 dwarfs $1 million today. How many Black Britons own a private plane?

The key question is: What excuses are we going to make for ourselves?

CHAPTER TWO: THE ASSAULT ON BLACK TULSA, 1 JUNE 1921

Preparing for Prom Night

On Tuesday 31 May 1921 the main concern for many Tulsan pupils was preparing for the big social event of the school year--Prom Night. Bill Williams, the 16 year old son of John and Loula, alongside his schoolmates from the Booker T. Washington High School, was decorating a hall on Archer Street in preparation for the school prom. Other students were rehearsing for the graduation. However, an adult entered the building and told the youngsters to go home and prepare for trouble.

The adult had just read a shocking newspaper headline that appeared in a White newspaper, the Tulsa *Tribune*. According to Dr Ellsworth the headline read: *To Lynch Negro Tonight.* According to other writers, it read: *Nab Negro for Attacking Girl in Elevator.* Professor Brophy thinks that it was probably the newspaper editorial, not its headline, that encouraged the lynching. However, no one knows exactly what the paper said because the surviving copies and microfiches have since been doctored.

What happened?

One day earlier, Monday 30 May 1921, Sarah Page, a White 17 year old divorcee went to the police with an incendiary story. She told them that a Black man, later identified as Dick Rowland, attempted to 'criminally assaulted her' in an elevator in the Drexel Building.

The police, however, found that Rowland had accidentally stepped on her foot, she slapped him, he grabbed her arm to prevent her hitting him again, and then fled.

Walter White writing in the New York *Evening Post* says:

> Chief of Police John A. Gustafson, Sheriff McCulloch, Mayor T. D. Evans, and a number of reputable citizens, among them a prominent oil operator, all declared that the girl had not been molested; that no attempt at criminal assault had been made. Victor F. Barnett, managing editor of the *Tribune* stated that his paper had since learned that the original story that the girl's face was scratched and her clothes torn was untrue.

The following morning, on Tuesday 31 May 1921, Rowland was apprehended and jailed. He was arrested on South Greenwood Avenue by two Black police officers (Henry C. Pack and Henry Carmichael) and placed in the city jail. Sarah Page subsequently identified Rowland as the assailant.

However, the Tulsa *Tribune* sensationally reported the event as a White girl had been assaulted by a Black man. The newspaper hit the newsstands on 3.15 pm that day. Its controversial headline or editorial about lynching had an immediate impact in the White community.

By around 4.00 pm, J. M. Adkinson, Commissioner of Police, told Sheriff McCulloch that Whites were talking about lynching Rowland that night.

One source further claims that Rowland was removed from prison to some other location that was never publicly disclosed. Halliburton claims that the location was actually the County Jail on 6th Street and Boulder Avenue. This seemed a sensible move since the jail was located on the third floor of the courthouse.

The lynching rumour, however, spread to the Black district (also called Little Africa). The Blacks phoned Sheriff McCulloch and offer to protect the jail from White attack. McCulloch told them they would be contacted if needed.

Around 9.00 pm, 400 White men gathered at the prison. Halliburton tells a different story. He suggests that the White men gathered at the Courthouse. Moreover, he thinks that they began to gather from 7.00 pm.

Which ever be the case, around 9.15 pm, a rumour spread to the Black district that the mob stormed the jail (or the courthouse if Halliburton is correct). Twenty five or thirty Black men gathered and went to the prison where they learned the rumour was false. McCulloch and the Black officer Barney Cleaver persuaded them to go home.

The Conflict Begins

A little later, a second rumour spread to the Black district that the Whites had stormed the jail (or the courthouse if Halliburton is correct). By now the White crowd had grown to perhaps two thousand people. This time 75 armed Black men returned. McCulloch persuaded them to leave but a White man tried to take away one of the guns. A shot rang out during the struggle and then 'all hell broke loose.'

It was customary among earlier writers to suggest that the Black men were highly armed but the White men were unarmed. However, when the first shots rang out, it was a Black man that was wounded. Another early casualty was a White man in a car a block away. He was killed by a stray bullet. Both Black and White men fled in opposite directions following this initial exchange of gun fire.

As the Black men hurried north to Little Africa other shots rang out coming from the direction of the courthouse. Fired by policemen or other armed Whites, the shots wounded a Black man in the abdomen. Ambulances were called and three arrived at roughly the same time, but a White mob prevented them from removing him. He died right there on the street. Less than a hundred feet away, another dead Black man was discovered. In the end, twelve men were shot dead: ten White and two Black.

The White men began to organise and plan a strategy against the Blacks. They seized arms by looting Black hardware, sports shops and pawn shops. Not only did they take around $43,000 worth of ammunition and weapons, but also more mundane items including bathing suits, coats, tools, tires and even watches. One shop, the Dun Hardward Store, reported the loss of over $10,000 in stolen goods. The mobs themselves represented a diverse cross section of the White community, white collar and blue collar.

By around 10.00 pm, the entire police force of Tulsa learned of the crisis and they quickly deployed along a line separating the White and Black portions of the city. They were given orders to stop Black men entering the White district.

By around 10.30 pm the police received a report that a Black mob was forming to invade the White district. White men volunteered to help the police and even offered the police the use of their cars. All told, about 500 White volunteers were given special commissions by the police to help them against the Blacks.

At about this time (10.30 pm), James Robertson, the Governor of the State of Oklahoma, contacted Adjutant General Charles Barrett, head of the Oklahoma National Guard, with the message that Barrett should phone Tulsa's Chief of Police or Sheriff to determine the level of seriousness of the crisis in Tulsa. The Chief of Police assured the General that the situation could be controlled without the use of troops. Despite this assurance, the General ordered the National Guard in Tulsa to be prepared.

Even before the General's order reached the troops, some 300-400 White men attempted to storm a military depot to seize arms and ammunition. Tulsa Guard members seem to have anticipated the General's orders and were ready for the looters. They dispersed the White mob by threatening to shoot them.

Figure 11. Little Africa on fire.

Tensions in the city continued to escalate and eventually the city officials agreed to accept the offers of help coming from the National Guard. Eventually, Major Byron Kirkpatrick sent a telegraph to James Robertson, the Governor of Oklahoma, with the supporting signatures of Tulsa's Chief of Police, Sheriff and a District Judge, which read as follows: 'Race riot developed here. Several killed. Unable handle situation. Request that National Guard forces be sent by special train. Situation serious.'

By 11.00 pm Blacks captured in the fighting began to be brought in as prisoners by the police and by the White volunteers. The capturing, jailing and later, the internment of Blacks, started a process that would eventually leave Little Africa defenceless against White attack.

Midnight 1 June saw Black and White men firing at each other across a railway track that separated the Black and White parts of town. By this time around 250 prisoners had been taken.

As fighting became more intense, Whites set fire to buildings in and around the Frisco Railroad Depot. The buildings concealed Black snipers.

From now till dawn of Wednesday morning, Whites entered Little Africa and systematically captured, looted, and burned buildings. Initially 60 to 80 cars formed a circle around the Black district. Each vehicle contained pistols, rifles, machine guns, and petrol bombs. Eight planes were also used in the assault. They were used as reconnaissance and to drop bombs of

Figure 12. *The Afro American* **covers the story:** *TULSA IN RUINS, BEST CITIZENS DEAD.*

nitro-glycerine--some say kerosene. Among the enemy were 'men in uniform' who carried oil and petrol into the Black district. The enemy stormed Little Africa killing, looting and burning. Locks were shot off doors, furniture was torn open, telephones and photographs were ripped off walls, flammable goods were doused in paraffin and set alight. Other looters blew safes and stole silverware, jewellery and other valuables. White women would follow the looters in, shopping bags at the ready. Fire soon engulfed the entire Black district. By 6.00 am, the Black district was invaded wholesale. Some of the enemy contingent included boys as young as ten years old. They too participated in all the horror and mayhem.

Little Africa burned all day Wednesday and continued to smoulder into Thursday afternoon.

An elderly Black couple were shot in the back of their heads as they prayed. The enemy pillaged the house and then torched it. Dr Andrew C.

Figure 13. The enemy setting ablaze a well-to-do Black home.

Jackson, 'the most able Negro surgeon in America,' was sent under armed guard to Convention Hall. This was where Blacks were sent for their own protection. While being conducted to the hall, a White teenager shot and killed Dr Jackson. Fifty or more Blacks barricaded themselves into a church. The enemy stormed the church but were unable to breach it. Instead, they set the church alight.

Mobilisation of State Troops

At 1.46 am of June 1, Governor Robertson received the telegraph sent by Major Kirkpatrick and immediately contacted Adjutant General Barrett. The Governor ordered the General to mobilise the troops at once, take charge of the situation, and restore the peace no matter the cost.

By just after 5.00 am, the General and 150 troops left Oklahoma City for Tulsa. Three hours later, some writers say four, they entered Tulsa and were met by 'fifteen or twenty thousand blood-maddened rioters.'

Moreover: 'All of the [C]olored section seemed to be on fire and desultory firing kept on between snipers on both sides while the Guard marched through the crowded streets.'

Figure 14. Burning of the Mt Zion Baptist Church. This structure was just 40 days old when it was destroyed and cost $135,000 to build and furnish.

In addition, there were trucks loaded with scared and partially clothed Black men and women under heavily armed guard.

Barrett later said: 'Twenty-five thousand [W]hites, armed to the teeth, were ranging the city in utter and ruthless defiance of every concept of law and righteousness. Motor cars, bristling with guns, swept through your city, their occupants firing at will.'

Martial Law and Internment

The General met with and discussed the crisis with the city officials who conceded that they could not control the situation. His next move was to contact the state governor James Robertson to request his authority to declare martial law. The Governor granted the General's request for martial law in a telegram that arrived in Tulsa at 11.29 am. The fighting and the consequent atrocities, of course, continued unabated right up until this time. So far, the violence had raged for fourteen hours.

The General, anticipating a favourable reply from the Governor, had already printed and distributed a proclamation which declared martial law. Martial law was officially declared at 11.30 am. Guards began to patrol the streets. The General also ordered the disbanding of the White volunteer units since they were ringleaders in the riot. Martial law remained in place until 5.00 pm on Friday June 3.

Most of the fighting had ceased by the time of the proclamation, but Little Africa was still ablaze. Guardsmen were ordered to help the Fire Department suppress the fires and to disarm unauthorised armed citizens.

Figure 15. Internment in Convention Hall.

Figure 16. Internment in McNulty Park.

In one instance, they confiscated a truck load of weapons and jailed 65 looters.

Thursday 2 June 1921, the following day, saw thousands of homeless Black families encamped on the hills surrounding Tulsa. The Humane Society (a local chapter of the Red Cross) provided food, clothing and water. Churches, schools and public buildings (outside Little Africa) as well as private homes became temporary accommodation.

All other Blacks were interned in detention camps. Many voluntarily sought police protection. Others were captured and sent to the camps by force. For example, one police officer captured six Blacks, roped them together and led them behind his motor cycle to detention at Convention Hall.

Located on 105 East Brady Street, Convention Hall became one of two main detention centres. By Wednesday midnight, 1,500 Blacks were held

Figures 17 and 18. Dignity and defiance against a great loss.

there under armed guard. McNulty Park, located between the 9th and 10th Streets at Detroit and Elgin Avenues, became the other detention centre. By Wednesday evening, 4,000 Blacks were detained there.

With Martial Law declared, the police broke up suspicious gatherings and enforced a 7.00 pm curfew.

The Aftermath

It is known that 120 Blacks were buried following the assault. In addition, numerous Black corpses were piled onto trucks and driven away. It is said that other Blacks were buried in mass graves and other bodies were dumped in the Arkansas River. The Red Cross estimate that 300 people died. It is thought that perhaps 50 members of the enemy also died in the assault.

Hospital and Red Cross records show that almost 1,000 people were treated. However, many Whites refused medical assistance lest they be identified as rioters.

Some modern commentators estimate much higher casualty figures to those given above. For instance, Pasha O made the following summary:

Figure 19. White couple using the destruction as a backdrop for a photograph. Other Whites sold photographs of the assault as postcards.

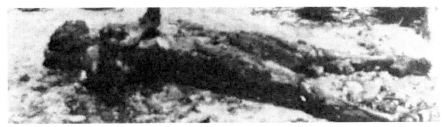

Figure 20. Victim.

The night's carnage left more than 3,000 Blacks dead, a lot of them were buried in mass graves all around the city. More than 9,000 were left homeless. Many of the survivors mentioned bodies were stacked like cord wood. Over 600 successful businesses were lost. Among these were 21 churches, 21 restaurants, 30 grocery stores and two movie theatres, plus a hospital, a bank, a post office, libraries, schools, law offices, a half dozen private airplanes and even a bus system.

It was found that special officers in the police were ringleaders in the killings. John Gustafson, police chief of Tulsa, was found guilty of neglect and conspiracy and was ousted on 30 June 1921.

$4 million worth of property was destroyed, the equivalent of 1,256 properties. Another way of looking at this figure is as thirty or forty blocks. For example, The Gurley Hotel, valued at $55,000, was lost, and with it the

Brunswick Billiard Parlor and Dock Eastmand & Hughes Cafe. Mr O. W. Gurley also owned a two-story building at 119 North Greenwood that housed Carter's Barbershop, Hardy Rooms, a pool hall, and a cigar store. All were destroyed. By his account and the court records, Gurley lost nearly $200,000 worth of property. Loula Williams, mentioned in the *Introduction* to this essay, filed a claim for $100,000 for the destruction of the Williams Dreamland Theatre and the Williams Building. Mabel Little lost her beauty parlour, her and her husband's restaurant, and her rental property. In total 4,291 Black Tulsans were made homeless by the assault. One Black women recovered items of her looted property from eleven different White homes.

We cannot overlook the personal losses of life. An old Tulsan inhabitant known locally as 'Dad' Otis Clark was 109 years old on his death, 21 May 2012. He was the last known survivor of the outrage. Clark was just 18 years old when the Tulsa race war erupted. He saw many people die. He remembered trying to get a car to help victims of the riot when gunfire came his way. Clark ran for his life, trying to dodge bullets. His family home was destroyed by fire. Moreover, he never saw his stepfather again. Clark believed his stepfather was killed during the outrage. O. W. Gurley, the pioneer of the Black Business District, lost more than property. The looters shot his wife.

Dick Rowland, himself, was exonerated in Tulsa. Sarah Page left for Kansas City. There are even rumours that at some point in the story (I do not know where) Rowland and Page had a relationship!

CHAPTER THREE: THEORIES AND ANALYSIS OF THE ASSAULT

Race riot or Race war?

Most of the earlier writers referred to the Tulsa assault as a race 'riot.' However, J. J. Wilson and Annette Wilson argue, persuasively in my view, that the correct term should be race 'war.'

In support of this view, Halliburton points out that the law enforcement agencies, the press and the public used terms such as 'prisoners,' 'skirmish line', 'concentration camp,' 'casualties,' 'refugees,' and 'reconnaissance,' in describing the assault. These are terms suggestive of 'war.'

What was the cause of this race war?

Halliburton points out that people at the time had very different theories as to who was to blame for the assault on Black Tulsa. Black and White commentators had very different views. Churchmen held different views to non-churchmen. Whether or not one lived in or anywhere near Tulsa also determined the different theories that commentators put forward. To cite Halliburton:

> Bishop E. D. Mouzon, preaching in the famed Boston Avenue Methodist Church, intimated that W. E. B. DuBois, who had spoken in Tulsa in March, might have had a sinister bearing on attitudes. The Bishop characterized DuBois as the most vicious Negro in the United States. Some 'authorities' believe the trouble was due to Negroes who had been 'preaching the gospel of so-called equality.' W. E. B. DuBois saw racism, economic competition and Negro pride as causative factors. General Barrett succumbed to oversimplification, blaming 'an impudent negro, a hysterical girl, and a yellow journal.' The Tulsa Ministerial Alliance stipulated that wholesale disregard for all moral and criminal codes, outlawing the Bible in public schools and immoral and uncensored motion pictures were to blame. Most Tulsa ministers made the riot and its causes the topic for their Sunday sermons. The Reverend J. S. Abel of the First Methodist Church--omitting any mention of possible [W]hite responsibility-suggested, 'every Negro accessory to the crime of inciting and taking part in the riot last Tuesday must be run down and brought to trial.' The Reverend Harold G. Cooke thought the press should have stated unequivocally that [W]hites were not to be blamed equally with the [B]lacks. Clarence B. Douglass in *A History of Tulsa*, blamed 'A lawless element of

[W]hite agitators, reds and bolshevists'. Tulsa police said the I. W. W. [i.e. Industrial Workers of the World] had been stirring up animosity between [B]lack[s] and [W]hites for months,' and that the Negro newspaper Tulsa *Star* had been urging [B]lacks to demand racial equality. Police and other 'authorities' also blamed the national organization known as the African Blood Brotherhood and its Tulsa chapter.

Theories worth considering

Walter F. White, author of 'The Eruption of Tulsa' 29 June 1921, was a staff member of the National Association for the Advancement of Colored People. He also saw some of the assault first hand. He offered two theories as to what happened, both of which, in my view, merit consideration.

His first theory is that poor Whites originally from Mississippi, Georgia, Alabama, Tennessee and Texas resented the economic success of the Blacks that outstripped their own successes.

His second theory is that the Tulsa Blacks denounced Jim Crow legislation, lynching and peonage and were perhaps too uppity (i.e. for White tastes).

Considerable evidence supports the first theory. At least 3 Blacks had fortunes of $1 million each. One source goes further and claims that 6 Blacks had such large fortunes. Several Blacks had fortunes of $25,000 to $500,000. A Black print house had $25,000 worth of equipment. The enemy contingent that burned this establishment included a White worker employed by the Black print house who earned a sizeable $48 per week! This example is evidence that racism is NOT practiced for economic reasons. It is practised IN SPITE OF economic reasons. Fortunately, however, this particular worker perished in the attack.

Amy Comstock, author of "Over There,' Another View of the Tulsa Riots' 2 July 1921 offers a very different theory, which I believe also merits consideration. One writer sarcastically noted that her account was written to 'relieve [W]hite Tulsans for any responsibility in the event.' Whichever be the case, she emphasises the role of weak and corrupt law enforcement. What she was probably referring to was the open operation of brothels, the alcohol sales (which was then banned) and the gambling parlours. There were also hoodlums, narcotics, bank robberies and store robberies. In particular, Little Africa was allowed to police itself allowing the area to become a cesspool of crime. (Readers should remember that the other American cities, such as Chicago, were hardly paragons of moral uprightness and clean living).

Moreover White Tulsa had even greater disrespect for the law. Halliburton lists the lawlessness that was generally tolerated coming from the Ku Klux Klan, the Industrial Workers of the World, the Working Class Union and the Knights of Liberty. These groups regularly engaged in whippings, beatings, shootings, 'wet ropings,' tar and featherings, and lynchings.

Coming to terms with the assault

The Oklahoma State Government passed a resolution in 1997 to produce a definitive account of the Tulsa Riot. They appointed as consultants Professor John Hope Franklin, probably the most important authority on African American history, and Dr Scott Ellsworth, author of *Death in a Promised Land.*

On 28 February 2001, the document appeared as *Final Report of the Tulsa Riot Commission.* One key finding was: 'Not one of these criminal acts was then or ever has been prosecuted or punished.'

'Another nagging question' says the report, 'involves the role of the Ku Klux Klan.' The report continues:

> Everyone who has studied the riot agrees that the Klan was present in Tulsa at the time of the riots and that it had been for some time. Everyone agrees that within months of the riots Tulsa's Klan chapter had become one of the nation's largest and most powerful, able to dictate its will with the ballot as well as the whip. Everyone agrees that many of the city's most prominent members were Klansmen in the early 1920s and that some remained Klansmen throughout the decade. Everyone agrees that Tulsa's atmosphere reeked with the Klan-like stench that oozed through the robes of the Hooded Order. Does this mean that the Klan helped plan the riots? Does it mean that the Klan helped execute it? Does it mean that the Klan, as an organisation, had any role at all?

However, one of my students believes that Klan blaming is simply a convenient deflection from blaming the involvement of the American government.

I believe more research needs to be done to settle these troubling questions.

CONCLUSIONS: THE LESSONS FROM TULSA

Part of a Bigger Story

The Tulsa achievement should be seen as part of a bigger story. Some commentators say that Durham in North Carolina presented an even more impressive African American business achievement. It was a centre of African American mortgage, insurance and banking companies.

Professor John Sibley Butler, a leading authority on Black American small businesses and entrepreneurship, wrote:

> Just as scholars today talk about the 'Cuban miracle' in Miami in the 1970s and 1980s, scholars around the turn of the [twentieth] century were excited about Durham, North Carolina. Just as the Japanese were able to develop economic success in California at the turn of the century, Afro-Americans were able to do the same.

Figure 21. John Merrick, C. C. Spaulding, and Dr Aaron Moore, founders of the North Carolina Mutual Life Insurance Company, Durham, North Carolina (founded 1898).

Figure 22. In 1887 John Merrick of the North Carolina Mutual Life Insurance Company moved into this Victorian-style home on Fayetteville Street, Sugar Hill, Hayti neighbourhood, Durham, where well-to-do Blacks lived.

Clearly Durham needs to be the subject of a later book. Readers should watch this space ...

The Historical Trajectory

The story of Black business successes in the western hemisphere begins with Paul Cuffe (fl. 1779-1818) who owned 6 ships and transported thousands of African Americans back to Africa. In 1900 African Americans owned 40,000 businesses. In 1908 African Americans owned 55 private banks. The first Black millionaires during this period were R. R. Church, who made it in property, and Madam C. J. Walker, who made it in hair care products. By 1925 African Americans owned 103,870 businesses.

Dr Claud Anderson says that between 1866 and the 1920s, African Americans made the most economic progress they have ever made in American history. At one time African Americans owned and controlled 20 million acres of land. Between the 1920s and the 1940s, there were Black broom factories and mattress factories. Nearly every city with large Black populations had at least two taxi companies and also bus companies. One particularly inspiring example was The Safe Bus Company of Winston-

Figure 23. Madam C. J. Walker.

Salem in North Carolina. Places like Baltimore had Black owned shipyards. Black communities had some of the best night clubs and restaurants. There were also two all-Black baseball leagues.

The story of Black business achievements ends with the likes of Oprah (the richest woman in the American entertainment industry) and Janet Jackson (at one time the third richest woman in the American entertainment industry).

The Three Types of Entrepreneur

In my opinion, Little Africa has much to teach us today about entrepreneurship and success. Generally, there are three broad categories of successful business people (i) those who largely INHERITED their wealth from their parents, (ii) those who largely STUMBLED UPON wealth from their own actions, and (iii) those who largely built wealth from their own SYSTEMATIC actions. I shall discuss each in turn and suggest how we can correlate each type with the Black Wall Street business people.

Firstly, Sociologists have long known that wealth is largely transmitted across generations through families. Consequently, Sociologists emphasize the importance that social class plays in passing down wealth from the wealthy to their children and their children's children. One supporting mechanism the wealthy use is high cost private education that is only available to the wealthy. This excludes the children of the poor and the middle class. Another mechanism is to induct the boys of the wealthy into informal but highly powerful social networks that are only available to wealthy insiders and excludes poor and middle class outsiders. I suspect that NONE of the Black Wall Street entrepreneurs inherited their wealth in this way but it is possible that had they not been destroyed, they may have attempted to build wealth dynasties across generations.

Secondly, there are people who achieved wealth as an unintended consequence of their own actions. These individuals had every intention of becoming successful and earning a living, but they DID NOT PLAN on becoming wealthy. Wealth was simply a by-product of their success that they stumbled upon. I suspect that SOME of the Black Wall Street entrepreneurs fit this category. However, George Subira, the author of *Black Folks' Guide to Making Big Money in America* has identified 24 sets of thoughts and actions that successful people in general use (see below). I believe that many people, including the Black Wall Street entrepreneurs who stumbled upon wealth, must have used some or all of these thoughts and actions.

Thirdly, there are people who achieved wealth as a PLANNED CONSEQUENCE of their own actions. These people intended to become wealthy and they took the actions necessary to become wealthy. Psychologists and Motivationalists speak of these individuals as proof of the 'Unlimited Power of the Mind'. Moreover, these examples of success show that anyone can be successful irrespective of class or background if they follow the correct principles. I suspect that THE REST of the Black Wall Street entrepreneurs fit this category. These entrepreneurs consciously followed some or all of the 24 sets of thoughts and actions, later identified by Subira, that successful people in general use.

What are the 24 sets of thoughts and actions that Subira indentified in the behaviours of successful people? Subira calls these the 'Fortune Building Principles'. I list them as follows:

- ◆Adopt a success orientated mindset
- ◆Take cost benefit risks
- ◆Have a vision of what you want to become
- ◆Be energetic
- ◆Have a money consciousness
- ◆Value asset building knowledge
- ◆Work hard and smart on your agenda
- ◆Be creative

◆Give up a piece of the action to others
◆Build a team for the long haul--lawyer, accountant, banker and craftsmen
◆Invest in property
◆Avoid high taxes
◆Keep and review records of transactions
◆Zealously control your time
◆Own your business
◆Build multiple streams of income
◆Live below your means and invest a portion of your income
◆Learn how to shop
◆Use OPM (i.e. use Other People's Money through borrowing)
◆Take legitimate advantage of other's misfortune
◆Use the media to constantly promote your brand
◆Delegate non essential tasks to others
◆Commit 5 or 10 years to your enterprise
◆Have a supportive spouse or no spouse at all

My objective in writing this essay is to inspire Black Communities everywhere to reproduce the success of Tulsa's Black Wall Street. To build this success, I believe that every would-be entrepreneur should read George Subira's *Black Folks' Guide to Making Big Money in America.* He believes that if a would-be entrepreneur incorporates at least 12 of the 24 Fortune Building Principles into their practice, they will make substantial economic progress. I share this view.

Moreover, I have produced my own more up-to-date ideas on entrepreneurship and wealth building that readers may also find useful called *The Seven Key Empowerment Principles.* See Part Two of this book.

BIBLIOGRAPHY

Books

The Booker T. Washington High School: Tulsa, Oklahoma, (June 1921 Year Book), US, 1921

Alfred L. Brophy, *Reconstructing the Dreamland,* UK, Oxford University Press, 2002

Charles E. Coulter, *Take Up the Black Man's Burden: Kansas City's African American Communities 1865-1939,* US, University of Missouri Press, 2006

Scott Ellsworth, *Death in a Promised Land,* US, Louisiana State University Press, 1982

R. Halliburton, *The Tulsa Race War of 1921,* US, R & E Research Associates, 1975

Hannibal B. Johnson, *Black Wall Street,* US, Eakin Press, 2007

Jawanza Kunjufu, *Black Economics,* US, African American Images, 1991

George Subira, *Black Folks' Guide to Making Big Money in America,* US, VSBE, 1980

Lee E. Williams et al, *Anatomy of Four Race Riots,* US, University Press of Mississippi, 1972

Jay Jay Wilson & Annette Wilson, *Black City of Gold--The Legend of Black Wallstreet,* US, Black Wallstreet Publishers, 2006

DVDs and internet pages

Cathy Ambler Ph.D., *National Register of Historic Places Program: African American History Month Feature 2012, Mount Zion Baptist Church, Tulsa, Oklahoma,* US, 5 September 2008

The Black Dispatch, 14 September 1922, Oklahoma City, Oklahoma, see http://gateway.okhistory.org/ark:/67531/metadc152402/m1/8/zoom/

Elimu, *Black Wall Street--Little Africa,* 2 October 2010, see http://pacingforward.com/2010/10/02/black-wall-street-little-africa/

http://www.freewebs.com/esmondcolvin/theblackwallstreet.htm

http://www.globalafrica.com/BlkHlcst.htm

Joe Looney, *An Old Tulsa Street Is Slowly Dying,* in *Tulsa Tribune,* 4 May 1967

Tariq Nasheed ed, *Hidden Colors 2:* DVD presentation, 2013

Oklahoma Historical Society, *SMITHERMAN, ANDREW J. (1885-1961),* see http://www.okhistory.org/publications/enc/entry.php?entry=SM008

Pasha O, *The burning of Greenwood aka Black Wall Street,* 3 October 2014, see http://www.eachoneteachone.org.uk/the-burning-of-greenwood-aka-black-wall-street/

The Tulsa Star, 7 February 1914, Tulsa, Oklahoma, see http://gateway.okhistory.org/ark:/67531/metadc72652/m1/1/zoom/

The Tulsa Star, 21 February 1920, Tulsa, Oklahoma, see http://gateway.okhistory.org/ark:/67531/metadc72786/m1/3/

Wikipedia, *Greenwood, Tulsa, Oklahoma,* see http://en.wikipedia.org/wiki/Greenwood,_Tulsa,_Oklahoma#

Frederick Williams, *Considering the Tulsa Riot of 1921 from a Black Writer's Perspective,* 1 November 2016, see https://thewriterfred.com/tag/black-wall-street/

The Young Turks, *The Final Judgement: Black Wall Street,* 30 April 2015, see https://www.youtube.com/watch?v=NdT8edPYQ7E

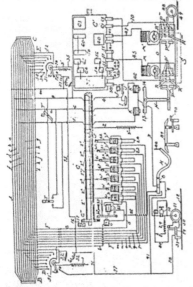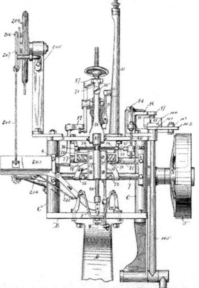

Also available.

Also available.

PART TWO

THE SEVEN KEY EMPOWERMENT PRINCIPLES

INTRODUCTION: WHAT DOES IT TAKE FOR AN INDIVIDUAL TO BECOME A FINANCIAL SUCCESS?

Experience and observation suggests that a successful Fortune Builder needs at least five things to build that financial success. They need (i) Inspiration, (ii) Correct Knowledge, (iii) To be using a Money Management System, (iv) To be exercising their OWN Personal Plan, and (v) To be exercising the correct Empowerment Principles. I shall explain each of these elements in due course.

My other ideas are taken from the five gurus that inspired me, George Subira, Robert Kiyosaki, T. Harv Eker, Robert Allen and Jacqueline Brooks.

George Subira wrote the incomparable *Black Folk's Guide to Making Big Money in America* (US, VSBE, 1980). I credit Subira for giving me the information and the steps to get 'off the plantation' into my own business. Robert Kiyosaki is the author of the radical *Rich Dad, Poor Dad* (US, Sphere, 1998). This book gave me a clear and objective target to aim for. T. Harv Eker wrote *Secrets of the Millionaire Mind* (UK, Piatkus Books, 2005). This book offered me principles that I could exercise on a daily basis to maintain my discipline and motivation. It also laid out a money management system that is of key importance. Robert Allen wrote the incomparable *Multiple Streams of Income* (US, e-book, 2009). This book outlines many of the methods that people actually use to make money. Finally, Jacqueline Brooks is a colleague of mine. Possessing a sharp and penetrating intellect, she continues to amaze and astound with her brilliant analyses and insights.

According to T. Harv Eker, there is a concept called the Principle of Manifestation. The principle suggests that the programming (or P) that you have received about a subject influences your thoughts (or T) about it. What you think about a subject influences your feelings (or F) about it. What you feel about a subject influences what actions (or A) you take. Finally the action(s) that you take strongly influences the results (or R) you achieve. Simply put: Programming leads to thoughts, thoughts lead to feelings, feelings lead to actions, and actions lead to results. We can show this symbolically as P leads to T leads to F leads to A equals R.

In this lecture essay, I shall explain and give examples of the importance of Inspiration. I shall detail what I call Correct Knowledge. I shall convince you of the need to implement a Money Management System. I shall convince you of the need for a Personal Plan of your OWN. I shall introduce the Seven Key Empowerment Principles. In short, I shall explain at a MINIMUM what an individual Fortune Builder needs to be doing to achieve success.

It is my belief that individuals who do not make it are missing one or more of these minimums. The missing element(s) show up in their practise.

What I present in this paper will help in reprogramming your ideas about financial success. It will also change your thoughts about financial success. Using the Principle of Manifestation it will affect P leads to T. However, what you feel (or F) about this information is down to you. What actions (or A) you take are also down to you. What results (or R) you achieve are also down to you. Only you can make these things happen.

My advice is ... do not waste this opportunity. You are always up against time and time waits for no one.

CHAPTER ONE: INSPIRATION FROM HISTORY

To achieve, Fortune Builders need to be inspired to achieve. One source of inspiration is our shared history. As the great African American historian, Professor Chancellor Williams said, the point of history is for the present generation to be inspired by it in order for them to 'go forth and do likewise.'

I have already written on *The Rise and Fall of Black Wall $treet,* an inspirational economic miracle of African Americans in the 1910s--see Part One of this book.

Here I present another example that readers should find equally inspirational based on research from my book *Everyday Life in an Early West African Empire* (UK, Jacinth Martin's SIVEN Publications, 2013) co written with Siaf Millar and Saran Keita.

Introduction

On 5 April 2012 *The Sun* carried an intriguing double page spread entitled *Timbukwho?* The subtitle asks *Rebels hit legendary city ... but where is it?* The article began as follows:

> IT is perhaps the world's most evocative place name, conjuring up hazy images of a fabled land at the ends of the earth. A recent survey showed that one third of Brits even think it is make-believe. But this week, reality bit in Timbuktu. Radical Islamist rebels seized control of the ancient trading hub in civil warfare that has engulfed the West African nation of Mali ... It is the latest twist in a settlement with an extraordinary history, a history every bit as exotic and strange as its name.

This tells us that early West Africa boasted a city called Timbuktu. It was a mediaeval centre of business. Why is this important? What happened?

Radical Islamists occupied the Malian city of Timbuktu by early April 2012. They threatened to destroy its mediaeval monuments and burn its old manuscripts. The world reacted to this threat believing that an important part of human heritage could end up destroyed. The French government launched Operation Serval to chase the terrorists out before they could destroy everything.

What was in those manuscripts?

According to the *Smithsonian Magazine:*

> The manuscripts paint a portrait of Timbuktu as the Cambridge or Oxford of its day, where from the 1300s to the late 1500s, students came from as far away as the Arabian Peninsula to learn at the feet of masters of law, literature and the sciences. At a time when Europe was emerging from the Middle Ages, African historians were chronicling the rise and fall of Saharan and Sudanese (i.e. West African) kings, replete with great battles and invasions. Astronomers charted the movement of the stars, physicians provided instructions on nutrition and the therapeutic properties of desert plants, and ethicists debated such issues as polygamy and the smoking of tobacco.

This tells us that Timbuktu was a university city with a rich surviving literary heritage that dates back to mediaeval times. The manuscripts cover law, history, astronomy, nutrition, medicine and philosophy. Says Tal Tamari, a historian at the National Center for Scientific Research in Paris, who recently visited Timbuktu: "[These discoveries are] going to revolutionize what one thinks about West Africa" (Joshua Hammer, *The Treasures of Timbuktu*, in *Smithsonian Magazine,* December 2006).

One of the surviving manuscripts that has revolutionised our perspective on Early West Africa was *History for the Truth Seeker.* A Timbuktu professor, Mahmud Kati, began it between 1519 and his death in 1593. His grandson, Ibn al-Mukhtar, added other information after his death.

What does the manuscript say? Kati wrote:

> It is customary for philosophers and learned doctors to recount the sovereign acts of princes and other great ones of the earth. In doing so, they act in accordance with the teachings of the Holy Koran, for to recall events that have been eroded from memory--to return to a time that has fallen into oblivion through human negligence--is to strive to make men of good will better citizens.

Which ever be the case, Kati divided the history of the West African desert region into the rise and fall of three huge empires: (i) Ancient Ghana, (ii) Mediaeval Mali, and (iii) The Songhai Empire. Historians still use this basic model.

Ancient Ghana

Kati recorded the typical night ritual of the Ancient Ghanaian emperor, the Kaya Magha, from the seventh century AD:

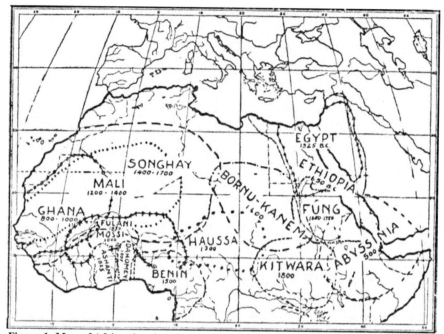

Figure 1. Map of Africa showing the mediaeval empires of Ghana, Mali and Songhai.

> The Kaya Magha came out every night after nightfall to spend discussing with his subjects, but he only leaves his palace only after they assembled 1,000 logs in front of the doors of the palace, under which they set fire. That light produced by the fire lit the space between the sky and the earth bringing light to the whole city. And then after that, the prince would come out and install himself over a platform of red gold.

Clearly the Ghanaian ruling caste had access to vast reserves of gold. A contemporaneous eleventh century source also alludes to the gold based wealth of Ancient Ghana. The document, written in the year after the Battle of Hastings, says the following about the Court of Emperor Tenkamenin, the ruler of Ghana:

> When he gives audience to his people ... he sits in a pavilion around which stand his horses caparisoned in cloth of gold: behind him stand ten pages holding shields and gold-mounted swords: and on his right hand are the sons of the princes of his empire, splendidly clad and with gold plaited into their hair. The governor of the city is seated on the ground in front of the king, and all around him are his viziers [i.e. ministers] in the same position. The gate of the chamber is guarded by dogs of an excellent breed, who never leave the king's seat: they wear collars of gold and silver (Al Bakri, *The Book of the Roads and Kingdoms*, 1067 AD).

With even the horses and the dogs weighed down by bling, was England representing like this in 1066? Clearly not!

A tenth century source says this about the relations between the city state of Audoghast and the ruler of Ghana:

> [The] king of Audoghast maintains relations with the king of Ghana. [The ruler of] Ghana is the richest king on the face of the earth by reason of the wealth and treasure of nuggets dug up in the past by his predecessors and by himself (Ibn Haukal, *Surat al-Ard,* 951 AD).

Not only did Ibn Haukal describe the ruler of Ancient Ghana as the richest in the world, he also visited the region and witnessed a merchant from the city of Audoghast writing another merchant from Sidjilmessa a cheque for 42,000 golden dinars. This all contradicts the common notion of a poor and backward Africa with no history.

Where did all this wealth come from?

International trade formed the basis on which the Ghana Empire stood. Through control of the caravan routes that connected the nations of the West African coast across the desert to the nations of North Africa, Ghana traded in clothes, fabrics, jewels, armour and weapons of precious metals. More importantly, they controlled three key products needed by the rest of the world: salt, ivory and gold.

There were camel caravans, donkey caravans, goods moving by barge and goods carried by head porters. Later empires would use these same trading networks.

Mediaeval Mali

The Empire of Mali succeeded Ghana and became the dominant power across West Africa in the fourteenth century. The BBC had this to say on Mali:

> In the fourteenth century, the century of the scythe, natural disasters threatened civilisations with extinction. The Black Death kills more people in Europe, Asia and North Africa than any catastrophe has before. Civilisations which avoid the plague, thrive. In West Africa the Empire of Mali becomes the richest in the world (BBC, *Millennium: One Thousand Years of History,* 1999).

The idea that Mediaeval Mali was the wealthiest country in the fourteenth century world was dramatically demonstrated by the actions of its most famous ruler Mansa Musa I.

He led a famous Pilgrimage from Mali across the Sahara to the Arabian city of Mecca in 1324 and took a caravan of 60,000 people with him. According to historian Lady Lugard, writing in 1905, Musa I carried over £1m worth of gold dust to cover his expenses for the trip. According to the website www.measuringworth.com, that figure conservatively equals £87,820,000 at 2011 prices. Musa I wrecked the Egyptian and Arabian economies by this trip. His spending created price inflation. The chroniclers of the time recorded that it took 12 years for economic normality to return to these regions. Could Bill Gates do this today? Of course not!

The *Daily Mail* had an interesting headline on Musa I called *Meet the 14th Century African king who was richest man in the world of all time (adjusted for inflation!)* published on 15 October 2012. The article began:

> An obscure king who ruled West Africa in the 14th century has been named the richest person in history in a new inflation-adjusted list of the world's 25 wealthiest people of all time. Spanning 1,000 years and with a combined fortune of $4.317trillion, only three of the list's 25 are alive today; none of them are women and 14 of them are American. Using the annual 2199.6per cent rate of inflation, where $100million in 1913 is equal to $2.299.63billion in 2012, Celebrity Net Worth's list includes familiar names like Bill Gates and Warren Buffett; but sitting at number one is Mansa Musa I of Mali.

The *Daily Express* followed suit on 17 October 2012. Their headline was *REVEALED: THE RICHEST PERSON EVER!* The article states:

> THE African king whose £250bn empire, says a new inflation-adjusted survey, was worth three times Bill Gates's fortune. 1. MANSA MUSA I--£249bn (1280-1337) Musa, whose title Mansa meant 'king of kings', ruled the Mali Empire (a large part of West Africa and including the city of Timbuktu) which provided half the world's supply of gold from three huge mines. A devout Muslim, he established Mali as an intellectual hub of the world. 2. ROTHSCHILD FAMILY--£217bn (1744 onwards) The European banking dynasty was begun by Mayer Amschel Rothschild, who was born in a Jewish ghetto in Frankfurt.

Thus two Conservative British dailies reported evidence that Mansa Musa I was the richest individual in all of recorded history. Even wealthier that the Rothschilds, Musa therefore sets the pre eminent example that all future Fortune Builders will be measured against.

The Songhai Empire

The Songhai Empire came to dominate West Africa in the sixteenth century as Mali went into decline. A sixteenth century visitor described what he saw in the city of Timbuktu:

> In Timbuctoo there are numerous judges, doctors [i.e. of letters], and clerics, all receiving good salaries from the king. He pays great respect to men of learning. There is a big demand for books in manuscript, imported from Barbary [i.e. North Africa]. More profit is made from the book trade than any other line of business (Leo Africanus, *A History and Description of Africa, c.*1526 AD).

Books were therefore more profitable than ivory, salt, copper, leather or even gold! The same visitor wrote:

> Corn, cattle, milk and butter this region yields in abundance, but salt is very scarce. Salt is brought here by land from Taghaza, which is 500 miles away. When I myself was here, I saw one camel load of salt sold for 80 ducats. The king of Timbuktu is rich and has many plates and sceptres of gold, some weigh 1,300 pounds and he keeps a magnificent and well-furnished court (Leo Africanus, *A History and Description of Africa, Timbuktu, Kingdom, c.*1526 AD).

Just as the rulers of Ghana and Mali blinged, the Songhai Emperor had golden nuggets up to an astonishing 1,300 lbs in weight. But there is more. A modern scholar, Lady Lugard, wrote:

> Systems of banking and credit, which seem to have existed under the earlier kings of [Mali], were improved. Banking remained chiefly in the hands of the Arabs, from whom letters of credit could be procured, which were operative throughout the Soudan [i.e. West Africa], and were used by the [B]lack travelling merchants as well as by Arab traders (Lady Lugard, *A Tropical Dependency*, 1905, p.201).

The fact that banking and credit systems existed is impressive. However, the data also highlights a weakness of the Songhai Empire. They should have ensured that THEY controlled the banking sector rather than leave it in the hands of the Arabs.

However, the West African golden age went into a serious decline after 1591. There was a sinister alliance between Sultan Al-Mansur of Morocco and Queen Elizabeth I of England. The English sold firearms and cannons to Morocco with which they invaded the Songhai empire and destroyed it in 1591. Following the fall of Songhai, the Slave Trade against Africa exploded in scale.

Africa has yet to return to her former glory ... However, never forget that West Africa produced states regarded as the richest in the world of their time. The region produced emperors regarded as the richest men in the world of their time. The region even produced an individual regarded as the richest man IN THE WHOLE OF WORLD HISTORY. One ruler even had a gold nugget that weighed 1300 lbs. The region controlled the gold and salt trades of the world and even had banking systems and cheques!

This information should inspire potential Fortune Builders to think that they too could 'go forth and do likewise.' If it was possible before, we should be able to do it again.

Synthesising the ideas of Brooks, Kiyosaki and Eker, I shall describe how the financial lives of the Agenda Setters (i.e. the systematic ones) and the Agenda Followers differ in two predictable ways: (i) how they make their money and (ii) what they spend their money on.

Firstly, the Agenda Setters (i.e. the systematic ones) aggressively over time grow both the quantity and the proportion of their incomes that are generated by their assets. Ideally they would like nearly all of their incomes to come from their assets and NOT from their labour. This ultimately provides the Agenda Setters with increasing quantities of self-directed time.

Secondly, the Agenda Setters (i.e. the systematic ones) aggressively over time grow both the quantity and the proportion of their incomes that they are able to spend on three key things: (i) their financial education, (ii) their assets and (iii) their personal agendas. Ideally, these three quantities should increase year on year. The Agenda Followers, however, are kept unaware of the importance that the Agenda Setters devote to spending on financial education. They are similarly kept unaware of the importance that the Agenda Setters devote to spending on assets. The one thing that the Agenda Followers ARE made aware of is the importance that the Agenda Setters devote to spending on their personal agendas: i.e. spending on themselves, their futures and other people. This is the type of glamorous spending that is reported on in the media.

Readers who are new to this subject should be asking themselves four key questions. These questions are central to this paper and will be referred to, explained and discussed throughout:

(i) What is an asset?
(ii) What is financial education?
(iii) Why is it important to spend money to build your assets?
(iv) How should you spend money to fulfil your personal agendas?

Agenda Followers, on the other hand, do not build or buy assets. The poor have no idea what assets are or how they can be built or bought. But this is not their fault, however. This information is largely kept from them. However, with the middle class, the situation is even more depressing. Sharks among the Agenda Setters encourage the middle class to 'invest in assets' that are really liabilities repackaged as assets. Thus the middle class are misled into thinking they are making financial progress when in fact they are being fleeced. Consequently, the Agenda Followers, whether poor or middle class, are completely dependent on their labour to generate all of their income. Not only will they work all of their lives, but their situation does not get any easier over time. The 18 year old is working 9 till 5. The 55 year old is STILL working 9 till 5.

Secondly, Agenda Followers place nearly all of their incomes at the disposal of the Agenda Setters. (i) They use none of their incomes on their financial education. The poor do not what financial education is or why it is important. The middle class are fed misinformation by sharks that lead them to falsely think that financial education is just learning about saving schemes and pensions. (ii) The Agenda Followers use none of their income on building and buying assets. The poor do not what assets are or why they are important. The middle class are given damaging misinformation by sharks. (iii) The Agenda Followers only enjoy the little money they have left over only after paying their dues to the Agenda Setters (in the form of transport costs, food shopping, income tax, rents, mortgages, debt repayments, household bills, etcetera). Even then, most Agenda Followers feel guilty about spending the little money that they have left over for their personal agendas. How sad is that?

Over time, the gap between the two groups of people in the financial world increases. The Agenda Setters enjoy increasingly self-planned and self-directed time. Crucially, should they choose to, they could subsist entirely on the incomes generated by their assets. This is also called 'passive income' i.e. income that is NOT generated from their labour. Moreover, they steadily get richer and richer over time. They enjoy increasing quantities and proportions of their incomes to be spent on themselves, their futures and their families, friends and interests. In short, the Agenda Setters make SIGNIFICANT, MEASURABLE FINANCIAL and LIFESTYLE PROGRESS over time.

In addition, the Agenda Setters pass down their assets and know-how to their children. Their children enter the financial world with a substantial piece of SOMETHING. This is why the children of the Agenda Setters usually far out-perform the children of the Agenda Followers. Thus cycles of wealth and success usually runs in these families from generation to generation.

With the Agenda Followers, however, the situation is very different. Whether they are 18 or 55, they remain just as dependent on the Agenda Setters. At no time does this group ever get to enjoy self-planned and self-directed time beyond the 4 or 5 weeks of annual holidays, the weekends and the public holidays. Moreover, their incomes remain relatively stagnant over the period and the proportion of their incomes spent on themselves, their futures or their friends, families and interests remains minimal. Most of their income in fact remains at the disposal of the Agenda Setters. In short, the Agenda Followers make NO MEASURABLE FINANCIAL or LIFESYLE PROGRESS over time. At best they are only slightly out performing a hamster on a wheel. They stay alive--to work--to pay bills-- to afford to stay alive--to work--to pay bills--to afford to stay alive, etcetera. The only difference between the 18 year old and the 55 year old is the SIZE of the wheel. The 55 year old has higher earnings but they also have higher expenses. Thus they have a bigger wheel than the 18 year old. It is ONLY in this sense that a regular Agenda Follower out-performs a hamster. Ultimately the Agenda Followers work efforts, lives, time and money is only serving the interests of the Agenda Setters.

In addition, the Agenda Followers usually pass down NO assets or know-how to their children. Their children enter the financial world with NOTHING. Moreover the only example the Agenda Followers set for their children is how to generate incomes from using their labour only. Thus the cycle of poverty in these families continues from generation to generation.

Conclusion

In order to become a Fortune Builder and get off the hamster wheel, you are going to have to copy the two key traits of the Agenda Setters. Firstly, you are going to have to build and buy assets. Secondly, you are going to have to implement a money management protocol to pay for your financial education, your assets and your personal agenda. Should you implement these traits, your financial and lifestyle situation will improve. You could begin the rebuilding of Black Wall $treet. You may even become the next Musa I. The rest of this paper will expand on these two key traits.

CHAPTER THREE: SHOULD YOU WORK TO EARN OR WORK TO BUILD ASSETS?

Having started to introduce some of the basic financial knowledge that Fortune Builders need to know, let me complete this process. I call this data the rest of the Correct Knowledge.

Robert Kiyosaki, the author of *Rich Dad, Poor Dad,* divided this book into six lessons. Of course, all six of the lessons are important, but in my opinion, Lesson Two is the key because it gives Fortune Builders a clear and objective target to aim for.

From recounting some of the highlights from African American history (see my *The Rise and Fall of Black Wall $treet*), some readers would like to go forth and do likewise and earn a million dollars, others may want a private plane, some may wish to dangle a $20 gold piece from a chain.

Using the examples from early West African history, some may wish to go forth and do likewise and build a £249 billion fortune, own a golden nugget weighing 1300 Ibs, or carry £87,820,000 in costs and expenses for a pilgrimage! But this all raises a question: What should be our target?

Robert Kiyosaki gives individuals a CLEAR and ACHIEVABLE target of what it means to be rich. His Lesson Two is: Know the difference between an asset and a liability, and buy assets. If you want to be rich, this is all you need to know.

Kiyosaki defines assets and liabilities in a radical way putting him at odds with all previous empowerment gurus. According to him, owning an ASSET means owning something that reliably flows money into your pocket at regular intervals, e.g. monthly, quarterly or yearly. An asset generates what Kiyosaki calls POSITIVE CASH FLOW.

On the other hand, owning a LIABILITY means owning something that flows money out of your pocket at regular intervals. A liability generates what Kiyosaki calls NEGATIVE CASH FLOW.

What are assets according to Kiyosaki's definition?

These include the ownership of Businesses that don't require your presence in order for them to function, Stocks, Bonds, Mutual Funds, Income Generating Property, IOUs and Royalties from Books, Music, Scripts, etcetera.

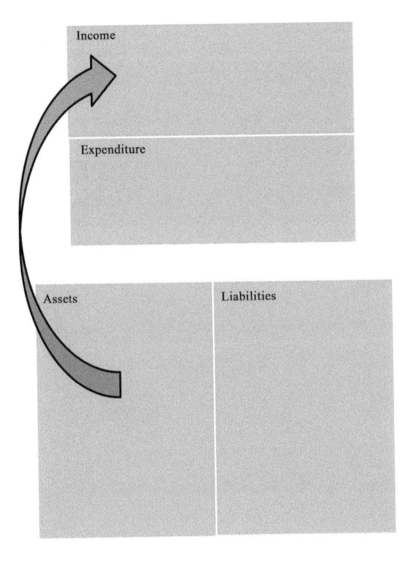

Figure 2. This shows the cash flow pattern of an asset. See explanation page 67.

What are liabilities according to Kiyosaki's definition?

The biggest liability is the ownership of non income generating property. For example, if an individual buys a home with a mortgage agreement, he or she will have to make monthly payments to repay that loan. In addition, the owner will have to make payments for the upkeep of the fixtures and

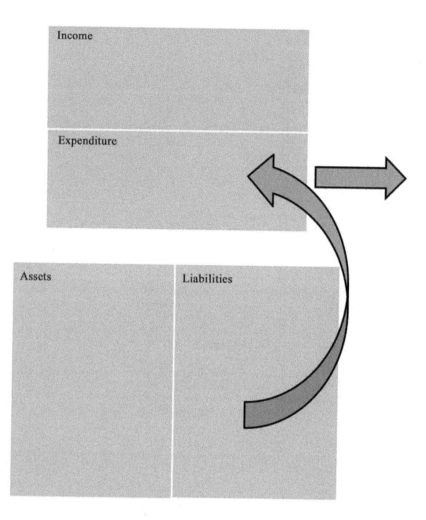

Figure 3. This shows the cash flow pattern of a liability. See explanation page 67.

fittings. Also, the owner will have to pay property and local taxes. These payments all flow money out of their pockets.

Another liability is the ownership of a car. A car owner will have to pay for petrol, taxation, MOT certification, repairs and maintenance. Other liabilities include having consumer loans and owning credit cards. Ultimately, all of these things require their owners to constantly spend money on them that flows money out of their pockets.

The astute reader may have noticed that the SAME item, property, can be an asset if you rent it to a tenant, or a liability if you do not rent it out but actually live there. Similarly your car can be an asset if used as a taxi or hired out by its owner, or a liability if you use the car for your own personal use. Another example is credit cards. If you know what you are doing, it is possible to use short term credit to your advantage and generate positive cash flow ... but this requires a whole new discussion (see Chapter 6).

So the key idea behind Kiyosaki's Lesson Two is this: The rich buy assets, the middle classes buy liabilities that they think or have been told by financial planners are assets, and the poor only have expenses.

Assets and Liabilities

These diagrams (figures 2 and 3) illustrate two sets of ideas. The top part of the diagram is an income and expenditure account. Income is the total amount earned by an individual from working, profits, interest, dividend payments, pension payments, royalty payments, rental payments, etcetera. Expenditure is the total amount that an individual spends including taxes, rent, mortgage payments, loan repayments, household bills, food, necessities and luxuries, etcetera.

The bottom part of the diagram represents things bought and owned by the individual. Traditional gurus call most these products 'assets'. However, Kiyosaki defines these things VERY DIFFERENTLY to most other gurus.

He says that ONLY the products on the LEFT HAND SIDE are assets. The ones on the right hand side are LIABILITIES. Owning the products on the left hand side (i.e. real assets) flows positive cash flow into your pocket generating more income. Owning the products on the right hand side (i.e. the so-called assets) actually takes money out of your pocket generating more expenses.

In an ideal situation, an individual should aim to INCREASE their quantity and sources of income and REDUCE their expenditure. Similarly, an individual should aim to INCREASE their list of assets and REDUCE their list of liabilities. In the next chapter, I will propose a Money Management System that facilitates these different purposes.

Cash Flow Patterns of the Middle Class

With typical middle class professionals, the level of income earned increases year on year. Moreover, middle class people usually work in

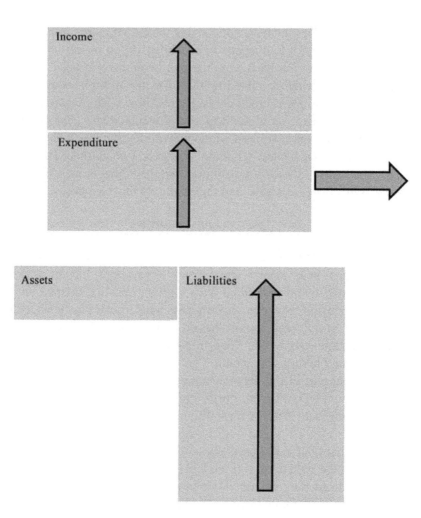

Figure 4. This shows the typical cash flow pattern of middle class people showing why they struggle all their lives.

professions where there are structured hierarchies to climb as the professional gains more and more experience. As they climb the hierarchy, they earn more and more income.

However, typical middle class people also spend more and more as their income rises. Usually this increased expenditure is spent on buying so-called assets, such as non-income generating property and cars. These are often financed by mortgages, credit cards, loans and other forms of debt.

Finally, typical middle class people are often misled by sharks in the

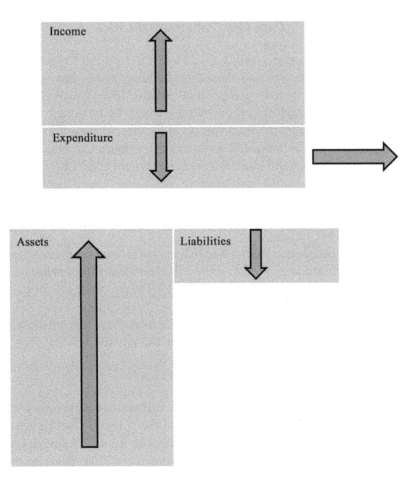

Figure 5. This shows the typical cash flow pattern of rich people. As their income rises, they buy more and more assets which raises their income over time allowing them to buy more and more assets.

financial sector into spending their increased income on liabilities that are presented to them as assets. Moreover, society at large expects to see middle class people living a middle class lifestyle that, without real financial education, can only be serviced by credit and debt. Few middle class people buy, create or build real assets that generate positive cash flow. This is why most middle class people struggle financially throughout their working lives. They are merely hamsters on bigger and bigger wheels.

Cash Flow Patterns of the Rich

The rich (or the Fortune Builders) know that it is crucial to spend as much of their earned income and their time building assets, buying assets or buying into asset systems that generate positive cash flow. With each new asset bought, created or built, a rich (or would be rich) individual earns more and more income. The increase in income, in turn, allows them to build, create or buy more and more assets. As more and more assets are built, created or bought, these assets generate more and more income. This cycle explains why the rich tend to get richer and richer over time. Moreover, they do not just earn income from working, they earn profits, interest, royalties, rents, etcetera, from owning the assets that they have built, created or bought.

Even rich people need to buy and live in non-income generating property. Even Fortune Builders need to drive cars. But ideally, they should use the incomes GENERATED BY THEIR ASSETS to pay for these things, NOT THEIR EARNED INCOMES.

Kiyosaki says that for every liability that you buy, you should already have bought, created or built an asset that will pay for it.

Who are you working for?

If you are a typical individual, it is likely that you are working a job or in a profession employed by someone else. In Jacqueline Brooks' terminology, you are following the agenda of an Agenda Setter. In practice this means that (i) You are working to provide for the business owners success and retirement, (ii) You are working to pay taxes to the government, and (iii) You are working to pay mortgage and credit debts to banks and credit agencies. You only get to enjoy your income only after you have satisfied the agendas of the business owners, the government, the banks and the credit agencies. These are additional reasons why the poor and the middle classes suffer.

How wealthy are you?

Wealth is redefined by Kiyosaki as a time concept. According to him, wealth is a measure of how many days forward could a person financially survive if they stopped working today and therefore stopped being paid wages today. Such a person would have to subsist on the cash flow generated by the assets that they own.

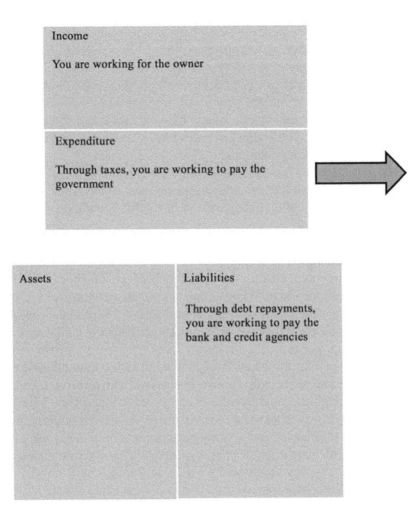

Figure 6. Who are you really working to enrich?

For example, suppose an individual's assets generate cash flow of £1,000 per month, but their monthly expenses are £2,000. What is their wealth?

There are a number of ways that an individual could generate cash flow of £1,000 per month. Individual A may own a property outright that they are renting for £1,000 per month. Individual B may have part ownership of a business and receives £1,000 per month as part of the deal. Individual C may have published a number of books and receives the profits each month for the sale of the books where even in the worst performing month they clear £1,000. There are many examples and permutations. Individual D may have a mortgage on a property costing £400 per month but rents the property for £700 clearing £300 per month. He may receive let's say £300 per month as the part owner of a business and may also have published books generating a monthly profit of say £400. Individual D is still generating £1,000 per month where property generates £300, business generates £300 and publishing generates £400. The reader can think of their own examples and permutations.

The key question here is: How long could any of these individuals financially survive if their monthly expenses (rent or mortgage, taxes, debt repayments, utility bills, transportation costs, food, clothing, necessities, luxuries) are £2,000?

The correct answer is HALF A MONTH. At the end of half a month, all of the above individuals would have run out of money and would not be able to pay their expenses for the second half of the month.

However, suppose an individual's assets generate cash flow of £1,500 per month, but their monthly expenses are still £2,000. What is their wealth?

Again, there are a number of ways that an individual could generate cash flow of £1,500 per month. Individual A may own two properties outright that they are renting for a combined total of £1,500 per month. Individual B may have part ownership of two businesses and receives £1,500 per month as a combined total from each of the deals. Individual C may have published even more books and receives the profits each month for the sale of the books where even in the worst performing month they clear £1,500. Again, the reader can think of their own examples and permutations.

As before, the key question here is: How long could any of these individuals financially survive if their monthly expenses are £2,000?

The correct answer is THREE QUARTERS OF A MONTH. At the end of this period, all of the above individuals would have run out of money and would not be able to pay their expenses for the last quarter of the month.

However, suppose an individual's assets generate cash flow of £2,000 per month, but their monthly expenses are still £2,000. What is their wealth? Is the answer ONE MONTH? Would this individual ever have to work again? What is the lesson here?

Provided that the individual's assets continue to generate cash flow of £2,000 per month and their monthly expenses remain stable at £2,000 this individual WILL NEVER HAVE TO WORK AGAIN! They will be able to subsist on the income generated by their assets INDEFINITELY. Anyone who achieves this has met the goal of FINANCIAL FREEDOM. This is ALMOST the ultimate objective that an individual should aim for.

The ULTIMATE OBJECTIVE, according to Kiyosaki, is for individuals to build, create or buy enough cash flow generating assets to cover ALL of their expenses (i.e. financial freedom) AND to have enough left over to acquire MORE assets (i.e. increasing wealth).

I expect that the majority of readers coming across this information for the first time probably own NO income generating property, businesses, intellectual property, NOR ANY OTHER income generating assets. Indeed, it is likely that most readers have never even heard of these concepts until they read about them here.

Your immediate objective should be to learn about the different ways that people generate income from assets (i.e. Businesses that don't require your presence in order for them to function, Stocks, Bonds, Mutual Funds, Income Generating Property, IOUs, Royalties from Books, Music, Scripts, Storage Space, Dispensing Machines, etcetera) and devote your time to LEARNING and MASTERING at least ONE of these areas.

Secondly, you need to enter that area part time and start building assets, buying assets, or buying into asset systems. Eventually, you should aim to generate enough monthly income from your assets to cover your monthly expenses. Once you have done this, you can quit your job (i.e. FINANCIAL FREEDOM). This gives you the TIME to search for and buy, create, or build even MORE assets. This increases your income.

Ideally, you should use your assets to generate the cash flow to pay for your liabilities (such as your house and car).

I recommend that readers who are complete newbies consult Robert G. Allen's *Multiple Streams of Income* as a way in to begin learning about income generating assets. As I shall explain later on, you have to bring YOUR OWN IDEAS and CREATIVITY to Allen's ideas to make them practically manifest.

Again, to stress the main point, every individual needs to earn enough money from their assets each month to cover all of their monthly expenses. For readers in Britain, this may mean earning a monthly income of somewhere from £1,500 to £3,500. Once this magical figure can be reliably achieved, that individual need not work for someone else ever again provided that their expenses remain constant.

You need to ask yourself questions such as:

♦How many properties do I need to own and rent out to achieve this magical figure?

♦How many books do I need to publish and sell per month to achieve this magical figure?

♦What quantity of financial instruments do I need to own, paying what percentage of dividends or interest, do I need to achieve this magical figure?

These questions give each individual a CLEAR and ACHIEVABLE target to aim for.

Breaking the Targets into Three Manageable Steps

To reiterate then, once a would be Fortune Builder or Agenda Setter decides they want to get off the hamster wheel or the plantation, they have to decide which area of asset building or buying they would like to master. Once you make this decision, you will have to undergo a lot of financial education in your chosen area. You will also have to undergo a lot of personal growth just to be able to confidently build your first asset, buy your first asset or buy into your first asset system. Do not underestimate how much financial education and personal development is necessary just to become skilled or knowledgeable enough to build ONE asset that reliably generates say £50 per calendar month.

To summarise then, your FIRST target is to build or buy your first asset that generates reliable positive cash flow. You will need to undergo a large amount of financial education and personal growth before being able to hit this target.

It is true that £50 per calendar month is not a huge amount of money, but it is STILL A MAJOR MILESTONE! Robert Kiyosaki says when you make passive income a part of your life your life will change. He is correct. From this figure, your next target is to scale up your activities to hit the target of financial freedom. One concept that may help you to scale things up is LEVERAGE. This concept is introduced in Chapter 5.

For example, a published book with a properly researched title and solid content plugged into a worldwide system such as Amazon might sell around 2 copies per day (one physical book and one e-book). This may generate profits of around £3.50 for a £10 book. This ultimately means earning £7 per day. Over a calendar month of 30 days, these sales may generate an average profit of £210.

Should our hypothetical publisher commission 10 such books with properly researched titles and solid content, this may generate over £2,000 per calendar month. This figure is high enough to reach financial freedom in most places in Britain. Being more specific, I suggested that for some readers in Britain, this may mean earning a monthly income of somewhere from £1,500 per calendar month (i.e. from 8 books) to £3,500 per calendar month (i.e. from 18 books).

To summarise then, your SECOND target is to scale up your asset building or buying activities to the point where you are financially free. You will need to stay disciplined and motivated to reach this target. I shall write more on this when I explain the *Seven Key Empowerment Principles.*

It is true that to earn a passive income of £1,500 in some parts of Britain or £3,500 elsewhere per calendar month could create a reasonable lower middle class lifestyle, but that is hardly the same as being rich. Certainly, our hypothetical publisher could double their outputs to produce £3,000 (i.e. from 16 books) or £7,000 (i.e. from 36 books) per calendar month. However, people who earn a million pounds per year are, by contrast, earning a staggering £84,000 per month! This is the equivalent of 400 published books with properly researched titles and solid content plugged into systems such as Amazon. While it IS possible to reach this figure, it is a very tall order and is thus an unachievable target.

Consequently, T. Harv Eker suggests instead that Fortune Builders should aim to build what he calls the Five Pillars of Wealth. According to him, individuals who are financially free should make it their lifetime ambition to build a financial fortress supported by five pillars. The five pillars are (i) a real time business or businesses, (ii) an internet-based business or businesses, (iii) a property empire, (iv) an investment portfolio, and (v) a job that you love to do that furthers your agenda.

The advantage of the five pillars idea is that it is much more achievable. To illustrate, the average quantity of income that a Fortune Builder should aim to generate from each of the five pillars is a more do-able average of £17,000 per calendar month (i.e. £17,000 x 5 pillars = £85,000). To use the publishing example, £17,000 per calendar month could be generated from 81 published books. This is clearly an achievable target that could comfortably be reached in 81 months (i.e. 7 years). A publisher would need to commission one new book per month. If you have undergone the financial education, you will know that this is an easily do-able target.

However, one key fact needs to be stressed. Do not underestimate how much financial education, personal growth and time is necessary to generate an average of £17,000 from FIVE different SETS of sources.

To summarise then, your THIRD or ULTIMATE target is to build your Five Pillars of Wealth. You will need to undergo financial education throughout your life in at least FOUR MORE AREAS before being able to hit this target.

CHAPTER FOUR: WHAT IS EFFECTIVE MONEY
MANAGEMENT?

Having explained the Correct Knowledge, I shall now make a case for WHY you should implement a Money Management System. I shall also give details of HOW this system should work.

It is important that any would-be Fortune Builder correctly manages their money. Money is NOT JUST the END GOAL of the fortune building process it is also AN INTEGRAL PART of that process. Correct money management is JUST AS IMPORTANT to the fortune building process as the building and buying of assets.

T. Harv Eker recommends a simple but brilliant system of money management. He recommends that you subsist on 55% of your after-tax income. This money should be allocated to buy necessities, repay debts and support your family. He further proposes that you actively manage the remaining 45% of your after-tax income. He recommends that you divide that income into five different accounts or jars.

These five different accounts should have radically different purposes: financial education, assets, play, the future and other people. Ten percent of the after-tax income should go into what he calls the 'Education Jar'. Ten percent should go into what he calls the 'Financial Freedom Jar'. Ten percent should go into what he calls the 'Play Jar'. Ten percent should go into what he calls the 'Long-Term Saving for Spending Jar'. Finally, the remaining five percent should go into what he calls the 'Give Jar'.

Thus 55% of your income should be dedicated to staying alive, keeping your family housed, clothed and fed, and meeting your financial obligations to the Agenda Setters. The remaining 45% should be DIRECTED BY YOU to financially educate yourself, build and buy assets, and spend on yourself and others to meet your personal objectives.

Without a money management protocol nearly 100% of your income is at the disposal of the Agenda Setters. Moreover you will feel guilty about spending any money on yourself when there are outstanding bills to pay to the Agenda Setters.

Your money is an integral part of the fortune building process. You must use it to fulfil many different objectives at once. Poor people use their money just to pay bills. Middle class people use their money just to pay bills, save and buy liabilities (falsely presented to them as 'assets'). However, T. Harv Eker suggests that your money should simultaneously accomplish SIX DIFFERENT PURPOSES. This is a bit like having a soccer team where each player has a different role. One player is the goalkeeper, others are defenders, others play in midfield, others are wingers and others are strikers. Using all of your money to pay bills is equivalent to putting all of your players in defence. Moreover, failure to actively manage your money is equivalent to putting the opposing team's captain in charge of your team.

We have already conceded that a proportion of your after-tax income should be dedicated to staying alive, keeping your family housed, clothed and fed, and meeting your financial obligations to the Agenda Setters. This means a certain proportion must be spent on shelter, clothing, food, taxes, transportation, and repaying debts. T. Harv Eker recommends that 55% of your income should be spent on this AND NO MORE. This raises an obvious question: what should you do if you really cannot survive on 55%?

You should aim to subsist on say 80% of your income and manage the remaining 20% into the five jars or accounts. This should be accompanied by a plan to eventually cut the 80% spent on necessities down to 75%. This is why it is important to budget and cut out any waste on non-necessary items. David Bach, author of *Start Late, Finish Rich,* calls this cutting out the 'Latte and Double Latte Factors' from your life: i.e. non essentials that have now become a part of the lifestyle such as lattes, meals out, breakfasts out, mobile phones, internet, satellites, bottled water, health club membership, etcetera.

This should be accompanied by a plan to eventually cut the figure spent on necessities down to 70%, then 65%, 60% and ultimately 55%. In each case, the remaining 30%, 35%, 40% or 45% should be managed into the five jars or accounts. As you reduce the proportion of your income allocated to necessities over many months of following this system, you will also decrease the proportion of your income placed at the disposal of the Agenda Setters. Now here is the good bit. As the proportion of your income spent financially educating yourself, building assets, and spending on yourself and others to meet your personal objectives increases, the larger proportion of your income is spent setting your own agendas. THIS MARKS YOUR TRANSITION FROM AGENDA FOLLOWER TO BECOMING AN AGENDA SETTER. When you implement this system and receive the results you will see the difference between moving forward and being a hamster on a treadmill.

Ten percent of your after-tax income should be allocated to your financial education. Nobody is recommending school, college or university education as a way to build or buy assets. These institutions primarily teach literacy, numeracy, how to logically reason, and the many aspects of culture. Instead of this, I am recommending financial education. This means education on the specifics of how to build assets, buy assets, or buy into asset systems. Assets include businesses that don't require your presence, stocks, bonds, mutual funds, income generating property, IOUs, and royalties from books, music, scripts, etcetera. I shall have more to say about financial education in the next chapter.

Ten percent of your after-tax income should be allocated to your Financial Freedom Account. Eker feels that this account should be saved for the long-term as part of a retirement safety net. I hold a different perspective. I suggest that this account should be aggressively used to pay for the building of assets, the purchase of assets, or to buy into asset systems. If you are successful and the asset generates positive cash flow, your income will rise. If you continue this process into the long-term, your income should CONTINUE to rise. This is your key objective. Moreover, the money available for your NECESSITIES and ALL YOUR OTHER ACCOUNTS or jars should ALSO continue to rise and rise.

The remaining 25% of your after-tax income should be spent in a self-determined way on yourself, your future, and on other people. The Play Account (of ten percent) should be spent by you to enjoy the finer things in life that may at present be beyond your reach. It is important that you enjoy this money. It should be spent and enjoyed without guilt since your necessities, financial education, assets, and your future has already been built into and taken care of by this money management system. The Long-Term Saving for Spending Account (of ten percent) should be saved by you for buying big-ticket items such as expensive foreign holidays, luxury household goods, and even a deposit on a home to be lived in by you. The Give Account (of five percent) should be spent on other people, used to support your religious institutions or charities, or just to give presents. It must be stressed that if you continue to undergo the financial education and continue to build and buy assets, the money available to be spent on you, your future and other people should CONTINUE to rise and rise.

One way to practically implement this system is to open different bank or building society accounts. For example, as soon as you get paid, pay ten percent of that money into your first bank or building society account for your education, another ten percent into your second account for your assets, another ten percent into your third account for your play, another ten percent into your fourth account for your future, and five percent into your fifth account to be spent on others. The remaining 55% stays in your bank account for your necessities.

You should use this money management system and all that it involves FOR THE REST OF YOUR LIFE. You should NOT be planning to retire.

When you are financially free, your daily concern should be about generating increasing amounts of passive income from increasingly diverse sources. T. Harv Eker suggests that you should aim to build the Five Pillars of Wealth. Even when you are 80, you should continue to dedicate a proportion of your income to your necessities and the rest of your income to the Five Jar System. If you have built those assets and your income has gone up and up and up, it is possible that your necessities may eventually fall to 30% OR LESS of your income. This leaves the remaining 70% OR MORE to be managed by the Five Jars System. Even at the age of 80, you will STILL NEED FINANCIAL EDUCATION since the world will continue to evolve and systems that make money today will be obsolete in the future. This will lead to ever new business opportunities that you should be taking advantage of.

CHAPTER FIVE: WHY SHOULD YOU UNDERTAKE
FINANCIAL EDUCATION AND PERSONAL GROWTH?

Financial education is the SPECIFIC EDUCATION of how to BUILD ASSETS, how to BUY ASSETS and how to BUY INTO ASSET SYSTEMS. Assets include Businesses that don't require your presence in order for them to function, Stocks, Bonds, Mutual Funds, Income Generating Property, IOUs, Royalties from Books, Music, Scripts, Storage Space, Dispensing Machines, etcetera. It is very unlikely that any individual has this specific information unless they grew up around it. Consequently, you are going to have to learn these specifics.

Another aspect of financial education is learning how to use LEVERAGE. I shall INTRODUCE the concept here, but you should research it MUCH FURTHER. Leverage is about how to do more with less. This includes how to maximise outcomes with small inputs. In the last chapter, we saw that a key source of your asset building money will come from your Financial Freedom Account. As we shall show in the next chapter, other asset building money can be borrowed from the banks based on your equity. Moreover, credit cards could be creatively used as a third source of asset building money. Leverage is learning how to use these relatively SMALL amounts of money to create relatively LARGE outcomes. As you study the asset building information TAKE SPECIAL NOTICE of the MANY WAYS that leverage could be used. Leverage works in very different ways depending on the asset under discussion.

Personal growth is the personal development that an individual has to undergo. It includes money psychology and what T. Harv Eker calls 'The Inner Game of Money'. Personal growth is necessary to sustain the new lifestyles that accompany the change from being an Agenda Follower to an Agenda Setter. Part of it involves identifying the negative aspects of your personality and conditioned emotional responses that are likely to self-sabotage your success. You should work on minimising and countering these negatives. On the positive side, it also means being able to programme yourself to become and remain disciplined. It means being able to stick to a money management protocol. It means being able to complete the financial education reading and programmes. It means being able to complete the actions. It also means being able to plan your increasingly free self-directed time.

It should be clear from what has been presented here that real financial education (on asset building, leverage and personal development) has little in common with the misleading nonsense aimed at the middle class about saving schemes and pensions. For example, this present author is a publisher. Books are my assets. A key piece of financial education I completed was the publishing course by Christine Clayfield. She teaches how to create books. Among the specifics involved in publishing a book are how to:

- •Research book titles and subtitles
- •Commission books
- •Design book covers
- •Typeset book interiors
- •Edit and proofread books
- •Draw up contents pages and indexes
- •Promote and sell books with no advertising budgets
- •Publish and print books
- •Publish digital versions of books

The above specifics represent the key asset building skills necessary to be a publisher. It is unlikely that anyone who has not undergone the financial education would have any of this knowledge. In my experience of studying publishing, this information can be taught and learned in less than two months. I believe that an individual could be ready to create their first asset by month three of studying the data.

How do you get educated?

There are several ways to undergo financial education. Here are a few:

- •You can read internet pages and watch YouTube videos on the business or asset type that you would like to get into.
- •You can join internet chat rooms devoted to that business or asset type and follow the discussions.
- •You can buy and read books on the subject.
- •You can go on long and short courses on the subject.
- •You can buy into the training programmes of the wealth gurus.

The training programmes are usually conducted in the major cities across the world and are advertised in the newspapers and online. The most typical venues are the conference rooms in the larger hotels. Very often the courses are free to attend but often lead to paid courses that are taught over an entire weekend beginning on a Friday and ending on the Sunday. Others are taught through webinars. Some are taught through a series of DVDs.

You should ATTEND as many of the free courses AS YOU CAN and NETWORK with like-minded people at these courses. The courses are in two broad categories: (i) GENERAL courses on personal development and money psychology, and (ii) SPECIFIC courses on how to build or buy a PARTICULAR asset type. Of the two categories, I recommend that you prioritise the paid SPECIFIC asset building courses although BOTH categories are important.

To illustrate the differences between the categories of courses, I will reproduce a very revealing conversation from a 2011 BBC documentary called *MON£Y: Who wants to be a millionaire?* Telling the story of the increasing impact the wealth building ideas of Kiyosaki and Eker are having on British life, the documentary interviewed a woman of Jamaican heritage called Janice Geddes. She had acquired the wealth bug and had attended the weekend courses. This is what was said in the documentary:

INTERVIEWER: To achieve their financial goals, wealth gurus encourage people to attend intensive weekend seminars.
JANICE GEDDES: The first one I went to was ... 'Unleash the Power Within'.
INTERVIEWER: And how much did it cost?
JANICE GEDDES: It cost £600. And then after that, they mentioned 'Wealth Mastery' and I thought actually that sounds good ... I decided I was going to go for that.
INTERVIEWER: And how much was that one?
JANICE GEDDES: That one ... £900 I think that was.
INTERVIEWER: Then what was the next course you went on after that?
JANICE GEDDES: A Bob Proctor seminar which was called 'The Science of Growing Rich'.
INTERVIEWER: Did you have to pay for that one?
JANICE GEDDES: No that one was complementary ... and in September of the same year, that was in 2009, I went on a stock course--its called 'Stock Market Beginners Course'.
INTERVIEWER: And how much was that course?
JANICE GEDDES: That course cost £2,000 ...
INTERVIEWER: Janice plans to make her fortune by trading in stocks and shares ... [Do] you know how much money you made?
JANICE GEDDES: I made nearly 2,000.

In other words, she studied three GENERAL personal development and money psychology courses and one SPECIFIC asset building course. It was only after completing the SPECIFIC asset building course (on stocks and shares) did she make any real money. I believe there is a KEY empowerment lesson here, i.e. you should prioritise specific asset building education over general personal development and money psychology education although BOTH are important.

Be warned though, some of these weekend courses may cost up to £2,500 at the time of writing. This is the maximum that you should expect to pay. If a course is more than this, it is probably a scam.

The Financial Education Scam Cycle

On the subject of scams, Jacqueline Brooks, my colleague mentioned earlier, pointed out that there is A MAJOR and CONSTANT PROBLEM with getting good financial education: The problem of The Financial Education Scam Cycle. The cycle looks like this. At first the money making system is underground and known only to the pioneers and their associates. Secondly, the information is revealed to a few students. Thirdly, the information is revealed to the masses but only after the money has already been cleaned out.

1. Information is underground
♦Someone stumbles across a system that reliably makes money
♦They perfect the system
♦They tell their friends and family
♦Others independently stumble upon similar systems that are equally effective

2. Information is made available to a few
♦Some of these pioneers teach courses on their systems where the taught information is now SOMEWHAT OLD but still usable

3. Information is made available to the masses
♦Scammers jump on the bandwagon and mass produce courses based on VERY OLD information as the centrepiece of their business rather than using the methods that they teach
♦There are even unscrupulous scammers that teach deliberate misinformation to misdirect their students
♦Some of the originals and the scammers write books on their systems but the books are mostly just adverts for their courses
♦The book information is now FAR TOO OLD TO USE and will therefore need a great deal of new creative input from you if it is to be used

Avoiding being scammed is THE biggest single problem of learning to build or buy assets. I recommend that before undertaking a course of study you should do as much research on the companies or individuals that run these courses as you can. Try to find out:
- ◆Do the course leaders use the methods that they teach?
- ◆How old is the information likely to be?
- ◆Have there been negative complaints about the courses?

When you attend the courses, take notes of EVERYTHING the course leaders say. Often the off-the-cuff comments that they make reveal more useful information than may at first be apparent. You should also be thinking of new and original ways of applying and synthesising the ideas that are different to what is being taught. You should also take notice of anything the course leaders say about using leverage and you should be thinking of YOUR OWN METHODS of applying leverage. I will have much more to say about this in the chapter on the *Seven Key Empowerment Principles.*

Conclusion

Financial education will remain unavoidably important for the rest of your life even if some of the taught information is a scam. Just because your assets generate positive cash flow for you today does not mean they will continue to do so indefinitely. Consequently, you will have to update yourself as old ideas become obsolete and new ideas come along.

To illustrate this, a 20 year old reading this paper may live for another 60 years. Do you think that the financial world of 60 years time will be the same as it is today? Let me ask another question: Will the financial world of 10 years time be the same as it is today? Of course not! Many income generation methods will have been dumped onto the scrapheap of history. However, new methods will always come along that will replace the old.

You need to stay as far ahead of the curve as you can. However, in remaining financially educated you have to be constantly vigilant of The Financial Education Scam Cycle. Finally, just because some of the courses are scams does not change or lessen the importance of financial education.

CHAPTER SIX: EXERCISING A PERSONAL PLAN

Having introduced some of the ideas of Brooks, Kiyosaki and Eker, i.e. the Correct Knowledge and the Money Management Protocol, I will now explain what should go into a Personal Plan.

A plan must show your proposed path 'off the plantation' towards success. It will include your financial education and your own ideas and plans based on it. It may well cover your journey for the next five years. It must also address the KEY ISSUE plaguing the Black Community--lack of 'means'. George Subira is the ONLY IMPORTANT GURU who addresses the need for 'means'. He believes that a Fortune Builder should consider working a second job to earn the 'means', as an intermediate step (see below). He believes that equity could be used to borrow the 'means' (see below). Finally, he believes that credit is a key way to raise the 'means'. Let me explain this here.

Subira argues that it is important to develop a clean credit history. Credit is a key to economic success. Many Black people have poor credit records and have moved at midnight to avoid keeping up with bills! It is a good idea to contact the institutions that you owe and come up with a plan to pay them. You should keep your bank and credit agencies up to date with any increases in your income especially if you are working a second job. You should pay regularly and on time and you should push for maximum credit limits. Accept every credit card that comes though the post. This is not credit for you to spend on silliness but for you to use as and when appropriate as a source of fast money for serious business opportunities. Subira says that you should aim for COMBINED CREDIT limits of MORE THAN 50% of your yearly income from your primary and secondary jobs.

George Subira in *Black folks Guide to Making Big Money in America*, 1980, laid out a personal plan that each individual has to version for him or herself. The seven steps of the plan, that you must draw up as a document for yourself, are (i) Do an assessment of yourself, (ii) Double your work efforts, (iii) Self education, (iv) Buy property, (v) Enter a business, (vi) Repeat all of the above steps, and finally, (vii) Buy your time back.

However, in devising your OWN plan you may add or delete some of the steps. You may even re-order some of them. They key point, however, is that it must be YOUR OWN PLAN that is UNIQUE to you and no-one else.

1. The Self Assessment

You need to do an assessment of yourself. This will help you decide which area of asset building (or buying) is right for you. You need to ask yourself probing questions such as: What are your strengths and weaknesses? What are your assets? talents? interests? habits? present job(s)? free time? goals? etcetera?

In my experience of working with adults, it is amazing just how many skills regular adults have. The problem is that most of us do not value our skills and gifts--especially if they have not generated any money for us up till now.

2. Double your Work Efforts

You should plan to temporarily work two jobs even if the second one is cleaning, a McJob, or overtime. There are good reasons for working these long hours. It enables you to:
- pay bills more quickly
- get a savings account
- increases your credit rating
- helps you to naturally budget (i.e. you won't have the time to spend money)
- working twelve hour days develops your understanding of business hours (i.e. the difference between thinking as an employee and an employer)
- buy the roof over your head with a mortgage agreement allowing you to rent out a room
- make the maximum and most productive use of your time

The most important rationale for working two jobs, however, is to smooth your passage off the plantation into your own business. Here is how: The chances are that you are working a job or are in a profession already. If you stopped working right now to set up a business, you would not be able to financially survive in the immediate term. How would you pay your bills? Where would the money come from? It is this fear that effectively dissuades people from striking out on their own.

However, if someone worked two jobs, they could save the extra income in the immediate term. Once they have built up substantial savings that could be used as a financial cushion, they could quit one of their two jobs and replace it with the business they are trying to build. While the business is in its infancy, they could subsist partly on the income from the second job and partly on the financial cushion provided by their savings. As the business that they are trying to build begins to become successful, it will generate income too. Eventually, this individual may be able to quit working their second job too and concentrate fully on building their business.

Moreover, a second job and the increased earnings generated by it make it easier for a Fortune Builder to implement the Money Management System mentioned in the last chapter.

3. Self Education

Subira says the next stage is to study and master data on the following subjects: Home improvement, property development, taxation and deductions, savings, and budgeting plans.

I would add that an individual should study widely about every aspect of the business or asset class that they have chosen to get into. Your knowledge must grow from that of a relative newbie to gaining near mastery in your area of expertise. You also need to stay ahead of the curve in this area for your lifetime. You must also grow in other areas of financial education to ultimately enable you to build and reinforce your Five Pillars of Wealth.

4. Buy Property

Subira sees buying property as the natural next step in the personal plan of an individual. Property is useful in several ways.

You can use property as a way of developing equity if this is necessary. It may prove necessary if your business requires a substantial bank loan in order to develop. One common question is: Where can I get the money from? The answer is equity.

Equity is measured as: How much do you own MINUS how much do you owe.

If the value of your property rises, as is often the case, the money value of the amount you own INCREASES. As you begin to pay off your mortgage, the money value of what you owe FALLS. Therefore the monetary value of what you own is greater than what you owe. This is equity.

Ultimately you should be able to borrow on the strength of the equity since financial institutions are likely to lend two thirds of your equity. Thus if your property is worth £300,000 and you owe £200,000 on it, you have an estimated equity of £100,000. On the strength of this, many financial institutions will lend to a maximum figure of £66,000. This answers the question: Where is the money coming from to develop my business? The money will be borrowed on the strength of your equity.

Owning property can also be used as an income stream, as mentioned before, by renting out a room.

Kiyosaki has his own ideas about property. He suggests that you should only buy property if it meets three criteria: (i) You should aim to buy it below its real value. (ii) It could be used as a source of rental income for its owner. Finally, (iii) it should be possible to raise its value by redecorating and changing its fixtures and fittings.

5. Enter a Business or an Asset Class

Plan to enter a business by identifying a business, an industry, or even a talented person (i.e. artist, musician, actor, etcetera) for you to work with (You may offer to manage that individual). You could also begin building assets, buying assets or buying into asset systems mentioned earlier. This is where the self assessment and self studying should pay off. At this point write a detailed business plan and think about how you can be CREATIVE in the plan.

This is not the place to discuss the details of a business plan. You can research what should go into a plan by searching online. Also you can get business plan templates from your local bank.

The word 'creativity' is NOT an open ended word with any meaning that you wish to give it. As I shall explain in a following chapter, 'creativity' is a specific Subira word with a specific Subira meaning.

As you move into a business or begin building your asset class, you can quit one of your two jobs, as mentioned above, and replace that job with your infant business. In the immediate term you will subsist on the wages from the other job that you are still working and on your savings. As your business takes off and generates income, you will no longer need to rely on your savings. Eventually, you may consider quitting your second job to give your business the full attention that it may need.

6. Repeat all of the Above Steps

The next step is to repeat some of the above steps. In particular you should do another self-assessment. By now you should be both a business and a property owner. Your position is now very different to what it was when you did your first self assessment. Several years may have elapsed in the meantime.

The point of this new self assessment is to get you to think of new income streams. You should always be thinking about increasing the number of income streams. Ideally you should keep more than one income stream happening at a time.

7. Buy Your Time Back

According to Subira, the ultimate aim of every individual should be to buy their time back. This is where your business (or property) empire has grown to such a point that you can afford to pay someone a wage to perform the tasks that you used to do in the business. At this point the business can operate without you having to be there. You will subsist on the profits of the business and whatever other income streams you have bought into, built or created.

Kiyosaki says that when you are financially free, you can and should use the time to buy, create or build more and more positive cash flow generating assets. T. Harv Eker says you should be aiming to build your Five Pillars of Wealth.

CHAPTER SEVEN: EXERCISING THE SEVEN KEY EMPOWERMENT PRINCIPLES

In previous chapters, I wrote about the need for Inspiration, Correct Knowledge, a Money Management System and the details of what should go into a Personal Plan. It was important that you thoroughly understood these concepts because these concepts form the basis for the main concepts in this paper: The importance of the Seven Key Empowerment Principles.

What are the Seven Key Empowerment Principles?

From researching the economic history of West Africa and the achievements of the Black Wall $treet community, it seems to me that individuals today need to address the following principles:

(i) Commitment to writing, exercising and evolving their own personal plan.

(ii) Commitment to *Rich Dad's* Lesson 5.

(iii) Commitment to creativity.

(iv) Commitment to personal growth and financial education.

(v) Commitment to discipline.

(vi) Commitment to action.

(vii) Commitment to defending their income streams.

However, there is the constant problem of choices and discomfort leading to people not exercising all seven key empowerment principles. This is THE MOST IMPORTANT and PROFOUND IDEA IN THIS BOOK so think about this carefully. If you tell people that in order to succeed they need to do SEVEN THINGS, they will usually pick the two or three ideas THAT THEY CAN GET WITH and just run with that. Moreover, they will usually pick the two or three things that they are most comfortable with and find the easiest to do. They will NOT implement the other ideas. My point is, then, all SEVEN IDEAS are EQUALLY IMPORTANT. In order to succeed, you must implement ALL OF THEM without exception.

I can promise you this: You will FAIL if you miss any of these principles out!

Empowerment Principle 1: Commitment to writing, exercising and evolving YOUR OWN plan

The past has gone FOR EVER, it is not coming back. The past can only be a source of Inspiration as I showed with the Economic History of West Africa and with Black Wall $treet.

Entrepreneurs have traditionally made their fortunes in property, shares, traditional small businesses, the High Street, the music recording industry, publishers, bookshops, MLM, Cash on Demand, FOREX, 419 scams and so-called 'business opportunities.' Some of these ideas are detailed in Allen's book, mentioned earlier.

What all these business ideas have in common is that they are all in decline! They had their moments when extraordinary fortunes were made by entrepreneurs. However, this is NOT true anymore.

For instance, how many people can look like Elvis, dance like Elvis, and sing like Elvis?

When this man's name comes up, many in the Black community routinely denounce him as a cultural bandit who stole Black music and profited from it. While this is undoubtedly true this is NOT the main point here. The question is how many people have successfully imitated him? The answer is PLENTY of people.

Go to any seaside resort and you will see Elvis impersonators who, with the appropriate dress and make up, are convincing indeed. So why aren't the impersonators rich? Elvis, after all, was popular. His dance moves drove girls to states of frenzy. His songs were massive hits and still sell today. So to repeat: Why aren't the impersonators rich?

All methods of making money are dependent on time, place and circumstance. If any of these parameters change or become dated, the method of making money will also become dated. This is why the past has gone ... FOR EVER. Consequently, you must write you OWN plan.

Why can't you beg, borrow, buy, or steal someone else's plan? Here is why: Kiyosaki, Eker, Robbins, Tracy, Reynolds, and most of the other gurus made it in the nineties or before, therefore their individual plans that made them successful reflect this. The world of the nineties was a very different world compared to the world of today. Therefore, if you copy their blueprints EXACTLY the way they did it, YOU WILL FAIL. You will be just as unsuccessful as the many Elvis impersonators.

Consequently, you have to write and exercise YOUR OWN PLAN and evolve it on a daily basis incorporating creativity, predicting the future, and using *Rich Dad's* Lesson 5. I will explain creativity and *Rich Dad's* Lesson 5 later on. I shall explain the importance of predicting the future right here.

Your Personal Plan should be your road map 'off the plantation' into your own business or asset class and ultimately towards acquiring great wealth. This may take you five, seven or even more years to achieve. As you implement your plan, the world around you will continue to change. In just two years time there could be dramatic new changes in the world economy, in the law, or even changes in technology. These changes may affect you both positively and negatively as you work through your five to seven year plan. Some changes may speed up your plan. Other changes may create roadblocks for you that slow down your progress. Some changes may present an even better opportunity for you to win in the money game than you even planned for.

We have to have the same courage that our early African ancestors who controlled the gold and salt economies of the world had before the age of the gurus like Kiyosaki and Eker. Similarly we have to replicate the courage of the Black Tulsans who built their own Wall $treet.

Empowerment Principle 2: Commitment to *Rich Dad's* Lesson 5

What is *Rich Dad's* Lesson 5? The lesson that Kiyosaki teaches here is that 'The Rich Invent Money.' This is where you can see opportunities that other people cannot see or have missed. In my opinion, this is the MOST PROFOUND LESSON in the Kiyosaki book.

Just as the Black Wall $treet business people did this, you MUST BE ABLE to do this!

Kiyosaki gives an example in property telling the story of buying a repossessed house 'at the bankruptcy attorney's office' that was worth $75,000 for only $20,000. He re advertised the property for $60,000 and sold it at a $40,000 profit.

This is an example of seeing a deal and 'inventing' $40,000 in a short space of time.

Why is this profound? You have to be able to do this with brand NEW business opportunities. You must also be able to do this with OLD and DECLINING opportunities as well. These include shares, traditional small businesses, the High Street, the music recording industry, publishers, bookshops, MLM, 'Cash on Demand', FOREX, 419 scams and 'business opportunities.' As you undergo the financial education courses and read the literature, you should always be thinking of BRAND NEW WAYS to apply the data.

However, in breathing life into these old and declining business ideas, you must use Subira's notion of 'creativity.' I have mentioned this concept before but I have not yet defined it. I shall do so right here.

Empowerment Principle 3: Commitment to creativity

Subira tells us that it is important to be creative. Being creative is NOT an open ended wishy-washy term that can mean anything. Subira uses it as a precise term that means three basic things. (1) Doing a typical thing but in a way that is unusual. (2) Doing an unusual thing in a way that is typical. (3) Doing an unusual thing in a way that is unusual.

Creativity can extend to how you design a product or service, how you advertise or promote it, how customers can pay for it, etcetera. Creativity can even extend to how you use leverage.

To quote Subira directly:

> Fred is a shoeshiner. People have to climb up on a stand to have their shoes shined. Fred has a spot in a shopping area with access to electricity. One day the idea hit Fred that people act like they're 'big time' when they get their shoes shined, so he decided to give it to them with both barrels. He built a throne for his customers. He spent a couple of hundred dollars finding a large English chair, decorated it with cut glass jewels, silk and even had lights flicking on and off. Is this silly? ... Probably yes. Does it create attention, curiosity and crowds? ... Yes. Does it create business? Yes. Does Fred make more money? Yes, more than twice as much because he charges more money, has more customers and works longer hours. Later Fred bought an old tuxedo and drew more attention. This is an example of a common thing (shoeshine) done in an uncommon way.

In the last few years, for example, Amazon, have shown great creativity in the world of publishing creating Kindle and CreateSpace books. This has created a revolution in book publishing.

Let me explain the difference between the OLD and the NEW. Back in the days before Kindle and CreateSpace, publishers would decide what book got published. They acted as gatekeepers. Nowadays anyone with the knowledge and skills can publish their books. The publishers are no longer the gatekeepers.

Back in the days, publishers would print books in certain quantities they believed they could sell (i.e. 500, 1,000, 2,000, 10,000, etcetera). They would have to store these books before selling them on to distributers or bookshops. Nowadays books can be printed on-demand. It is unnecessary to print hundreds and thousands of copies and then store them.

Back in the days, publishers would sell books primarily to bookshops. Nowadays books can be bought online. This is why bookshops themselves are in terminal decline as a type of business, as is much of the High Street.

Finally, to sell books you had to be a 'big name' author. Having the 'name' was necessary for bookshops to agree to buy and stock your books. This too has changed. Selling online has given the 'small time' entrepreneur almost as much opportunity to compete with the 'big boys' in selling their books.

How can all of this be turned into a NEW creativity model? OLD and DECLINING ideas such as book publishing, 'Cash on Demand', information publishing and internet marketing can be combined to create NEW ways of doing business and making fortunes. I believe that this is true of ALL the old and declining methods.

You have to come up with YOUR OWN IDEAS whether it is with NEW business models or the OLD ones such as shares, traditional small businesses, the High Street, the music recording industry, publishers, bookshops, MLM, 'Cash on Demand', FOREX, 419 scams and 'business opportunities.' Even if you choose to buy into some other guru's business model, you STILL have to exercise creativity and produce YOUR OWN IDEAS. Remember, the information they teach will be old by the time it gets to you. You will FAIL if you copy their blueprints EXACTLY the same way they did it.

Empowerment Principle 4: Commitment to personal growth and financial education

T. Harv Eker's Wealth File 9 from his book *Secrets of the Millionaire Mind* says the following: 'Some people are bigger than their problems. Others are smaller than their problems.'

According to Eker, successful people fall into the first group. Unsuccessful people fall into the second group.

To illustrate this, he gives the example of a scale from 1 to 10 where 1 is the lowest in terms of strength and character and 10 is the highest. Suppose you are at level 3 in terms of strength and character but you are confronted with a level 7 problem. Compared to you, is this a big or a little problem?

We would all agree that this is a big problem. It is more than twice as big as what you can comfortably cope with.

However, suppose you have grown to become a level 8 person in terms of strength and character and, again, you are still confronted with a level 7 problem. Compared to you, is this a big or a little problem?

In this case, however, you can easily cope with the problem. It is something that you can easily confront or fix.

Finally, let us suppose you have grown to become a level 10 person in terms of strength and character and, again, you are confronted with a level 7 problem. Compared to you, is this a big or a little problem?

Clearly the problem is no big deal for you. So Eker's principle is this: The size of the problem is never the issue. What matters is the size of you.

For example, was anti-Black racism a bigger problem in 1921 or now? Does our community have any real excuses compared to the Black Wall $treet business people?

So how do you grow in strength and character? Kiyosaki calls growth 'The Leverage of Your Habits' and calls on success seekers to constantly expand their contexts and content by constant learning.

There are several ways to learn and grow:

♦You can read internet pages and watch YouTube videos on the business or asset type that you would like to get into.

♦You can join internet chat rooms devoted to that business or asset type and follow the discussions.

♦You can buy and read books on the subject.

♦You can go on long and short courses on the subject.

♦You can buy into the training programmes of the wealth gurus.

♦You can identify people who are already in the business or already trade the income generating asset class that you want to master. You can meet with them and learn from them on a weekly basis while taking them out to dinner.

♦You can actually get practical by starting a business part time or trading the asset type part time. In both cases you can learn on the job.

♦Finally, you can combine ALL of these learning methods. This is what I would personally recommend.

However, do not underestimate (i) the quantity of new information that you will have to learn, and (ii) how your own comforting beliefs and emotions will be challenged and confronted by the information.

Moreover, do not underestimate the skill level that you will have to develop in order to compete. You have to go from newbie to professional in your chosen field. You will also have to learn to apply leverage in chosen field. This may take anything from two months to ten years of constant learning and growth. Then you have to consider the large amount of lifelong education and growth necessary to build the Five Pillars of Wealth.

Moreover getting financially educated will cost you. This is why you must stick to the Money Management System to raise the money for your education.

Is your comfort zone a trap? Eker points out that there is a difference between being in your comfort zone and being in discomfort. If you are leading a level 6 life and you want to move to a level 10 life, 6 and below are in your comfort zone but 7 and above are outside your comfort zone. Poor and middle-class people do not like being uncomfortable.

To grow as a person you have to expand your comfort zone and become comfortable outside of that zone. I give the example of Asian businessmen who have cornered the market in certain aspects of African hair care. Not only have men cornered a market in women's hair care, but men who have hair, very different to African hair, have managed to corner this market. Imagine how far outside of their comfort zone these businessmen have had to operate in. I give this example to make the point. This is not the place to generate arguments over the rights and wrongs of Asian men controlling African hair care.

Eker's principle is this: The only time you're actually growing is when you are uncomfortable. You cannot be comfortable and grow. However, to continually grow, you need to have DISCIPLINE.

Empowerment Principle 5: Commitment to discipline

Discipline is the psychological basis for personal growth. Only with discipline is it possible to carry out the different principles outlined here.

What is discipline? Discipline involves strict repeated habit forming actions in the areas of time management, learning, productivity, advertising, networking, saving, budgeting, investing, etcetera. Discipline involves repeated habit forming actions to follow through on the seven empowerment principles given here. A key way to combine many of these branches of discipline is to implement the Money Management System mentioned in an earlier chapter.

How do you become disciplined? Different gurus have their own ideas on how to become disciplined. No doubt you have your own ideas on this too. Subira calls for active blueprinting. Eker calls for ritualisation.

With active blueprinting, Subira says you must write down and redesign you by setting goals for the *intellectual* you, the *physical* you, the *financial* you, the *spiritual* you, the *parental* you, the *mate-lover* you, etcetera. You must work on these goals daily to improve and evolve into the new you.

Eker says there is a difference between a DECLARATION and an AFFIRMATION. An AFFIRMATION is a positive statement asserting that the goal you wish to achieve is already happening. However, a DECLARATION is to state an official intention to undertake a particular course of action or to adopt a particular status.

Moreover, to verbally state a declaration is to make a formal statement of energy into the universe. It includes all the actions you must take to make your intentions a reality. Eker says the following: "I recommend that you state your declarations aloud each morning and each evening. Doing your declarations while looking into a mirror will accelerate the process even more."

To give a worked example: Place your hand on your heart and say the following declaration aloud. "My ability to absorb into my inner world the seven key empowerment principles will create my outer reality." Now touch ahead and say "I have a millionaire mind."

Eker suggests having daily declarations written and posted all around the house for you to see them and be reminded of them each and every day.

Many motivationalists offer courses on money psychology, personal development and the link to discipline. You may find some of these courses helpful in identifying your own self-sabotaging emotions, thoughts and behaviours. However, the ritualisation or active blueprinting must be followed by repeated habit forming ACTIONS.

Empowerment Principle 6: Commitment to action

In Eker's Wealth File 3 from his book, he says: 'Some people are committed to being rich. Others just want to be rich.'

According to Eker, successful people fall into the first group. Unsuccessful people fall into the second group.

Eker states that as long as what you are attempting to do is legal, moral, and ethical, the rich will do WHATEVER IT TAKES to build wealth. They do not send confused mixed messages into the universe. Poor people, however, send confused mixed messages into the universe.

A mixed message is where someone says they want to be rich but when you ask that same person "what do they think of rich people?" They claim rich people are greedy, spoilt and negative. If you asked that person "do you want to be greedy, spoilt and negative?" They say "no." This is a mixed message. It demonstrates that they do not really want to be rich!

According to Eker, there are three levels of wanting. I WANT to be rich. I CHOOSE to be rich. I COMMIT to being rich. Committing to being rich means you must hold absolutely nothing back in your struggle for success. It is the way of the warrior. There cannot be any excuses, no ifs, no buts and certainly no maybes. 50 Cent calls it: 'get rich or die trying.' The keyword is UNRESERVEDLY holding nothing back.

What is your commitment to being successful? Eker asks: Are you willing to commit to working round the clock for seven days a week and lose the majority of your weekends? Are you willing to make the immediate term sacrifice of seeing your family and friends? Are you willing to risk your savings and start up capital with no cast iron guarantee that there will ever be a return on your efforts?

In all these cases, successful people are prepared to do this. What is stopping you? Is it fear? Is fear stopping you from taking action?

Eker's Wealth File 16 says: 'Some people act in spite of fear. Some people let fear stop them.'

According to Eker, successful people fall into the first group. Unsuccessful people fall into the second group.

I ask the question: Who should have had more fear, Black Tulsans in 1921, or you in 2016? Clearly if the Black Tulsans achieved what they achieved, we do not have any valid excuses today.

Eker defines fear as: 'Anticipation of Pain' and asks "Is this a present tense or future tense thing?" Is the pain GUARANTEED to happen? Clearly it is NOT guaranteed to happen.

I ask: What happens when you wait for the fear to go away? Will you EVER take action? Remember our model that says that P leads to T leads to F leads to A equals R. If fear stops you from taking action there will be NO RESULTS. Eker says: The fear will never go away. All you can do is 'tame the cobra' but JUST DO IT ANYWAY!

Empowerment Principle 7: Commitment to defending your income streams

All methods of making money have one thing in common. They are dependent on time, place and circumstance. Consequently, they will ALL date. They will all stop making money at some point. This is why you have to defend your income streams. Looking at our history from the Songhai Empire to Black Wall $treet, WE CONSISTENTLY FAILED TO DEFEND what we had. If you don't defend, you lose. It is as simple as that.

In order to defend, you must be constantly ahead of the curve to stop this from affecting you. You must continue to learn, grow, be creative and remain disciplined. You have to keep on monitoring your present income streams and keep on looking to buy, build or create new ones. You should be just as concerned about this now as when you are 80!

If you want to know how the future will look, keep on looking at the world through the eyes of the 15 year olds. Nearly all of them have websites. Moreover, nearly all of them use social media like Facebook and Instagram. We can therefore deduce that in the future, everybody will have a website. What this means for you in the immediate term is that your ability to master the internet or any other new social media will be a marketing skill of the future.

But be warned ... This TOO will become outdated!

SUMMARY

We have looked at Inspiration and why it is important. I have shown that early West African peoples in mediaeval times amassed great wealth that has not been equalled by anyone since. Elsewhere I have shown how African Americans in Tulsa built a business district nicknamed 'The Negro Wall $treet.' These examples should inspire Fortune Builders of today to go forth and do likewise.

We have addressed the need for Correct Knowledge and what it entails. Correct knowledge means understanding the two sets of differences between the Agenda Setters and the Agenda Followers in how they handle money. Correct knowledge also gives individuals clear financial targets of what to aim for. For most readers in the UK, this means being able to generate income from your assets that reach the magical figure of from £1,500 to £3,500 per calendar month.

I have made a case for why you need to implement a Money Management System. I have shown that this system is an integral part of the Fortune Building process.

I have made a case for why you need to write, exercise and evolve your own Personal Plan. This plan must be individual to you. You cannot copy it from anyone else, nor can you buy it from a motivational guru. The gurus can only sell you old to very old information. It can only be updated and manifested by you.

Finally, I have spelled out the details of the Seven Key Empowerment Principles and how to use them. As I stressed before, ALL SEVEN LESSONS are ESSENTIAL. Miss any one of these out and you are destined to fail.

Remember the Principle of Manifestation that states: Programming leads to thoughts, thoughts lead to feelings, feelings lead to actions, and actions lead to results (i.e. P leads to T leads to F leads to A equals R). The content in this paper will affect the P leads to T. However the F leads to A equals R is down to you! I can give the content but ONLY YOU can make things happen. Your next steps should be to: (i) Implement the Money Management System straight away, (ii) Implement the Seven Key

Empowerment Principles to guide your financial education and personal growth, and (iii) Draw up your Personal Plan.

As I said in the Introduction ... do not waste this opportunity. You are always up against time and time waits for no one.

BIBLIOGRAPHY

Do not consider this, or ANY book, to be the final word on the subject. It is important to keep on learning and growing. In writing this paper, I used the following books, all of which I greatly recommend.

Robert G. Allen, *Multiple Streams of Income,* 2009

David Bach, *Start Late, Finish Rich,* UK, Penguin Books, 2005

T. Harv Eker, *Secrets of the Millionaire Mind,* UK, Piatkus Books, 2005

Vanessa Engle (producer), *MON£Y: Who wants to be a millionaire?* UK, BBC TV Documentary, 2011

Robert Kiyosaki, *Retire Young, Retire Rich,* US, Sphere, 2002

Robert Kiyosaki, *Rich Dad, Poor Dad,* US, Sphere, 1998

Jawanza Kunjufu, *Black Economics,* US, African American Images, 1991

George Subira, *Black Folks' Guide to Business Success,* US, VSBE, 1986

George Subira, *Black Folks' Guide to Making Big Money in America,* US, VSBE, 1980

Sources used for the history section

Chancellor Williams, *The Destruction of Black Civilization,* US, Third World Press, 1987

Robin Walker, Siaf Millar & Saran Keita, *Everyday Life in an Early West African Empire,* UK, Jacinth Martin's SIVEN Publishing, 2013

PART THREE

THE AUTHOR

ROBIN WALKER

Biography

Robin Walker 'The Black History Man' was born in London but has also lived in Jamaica. He attended the London School of Economics and Political Science where he read Economics.

In 1991 and 1992, he studied African World Studies with the brilliant Dr Femi Biko and later with Mr Kenny Bakie. Between 1993 and 1994, he trained as a secondary school teacher at Edge Hill College (linked to the University of Lancaster).

Since 1992 and up to the present period, Robin Walker has lectured in adult education, taught university short courses, and chaired conferences in African World Studies, Egyptology and Black History. The venues have been in Toxteth (Liverpool), Manchester, Leeds, Bradford, Huddersfield, Birmingham, Cambridge, Buckinghamshire and London.

Since 1994 he has taught Economics, Business & Finance, Mathematics, Information Communications Technology, PSHE/Citizenship and also History at various schools in London and Essex.

In 1999 he wrote *Classical Splendour: Roots of Black History* published in the UK by Bogle L'Ouverture Publications. In the same year, he co-authored (with Siaf Millar) *The West African Empire of Songhai*, a textbook used by many schools across the country.

In 2000 he co-authored (again with Siaf Millar) *Sword, Seal and Koran*, another book on the Songhai Empire of West Africa.

In 2006 he wrote the seminal *When We Ruled*. This was the most advanced synthesis on Ancient and Mediaeval African history ever written by a single author. It was a massive expansion of his earlier book *Classical Splendour: Roots of Black History* and established his reputation as the leading Black History educational service provider.

In 2008 he wrote *Before The Slave Trade,* a highly pictorial companion volume to *When We Ruled*.

Between 2011 and 2013 he wrote a series of e-books for download sold through Amazon Kindle.

In 2013 he co-authored (with Siaf Millar and Saran Keita) *Everyday Life In An Early West African Empire*. It was a massive expansion on the earlier book *Sword, Seal & Koran*. He updated *When We Ruled* by incorporating nearly all the images from *Before The Slave Trade*. He also wrote a trilogy of science books entitled *Blacks and Science Volumes One, Two* and *Three*.

In 2014 he wrote *The Rise and Fall of Black Wall $treet and the Seven Key Empowerment Principles, Blacks and Religion Volume One* and *If you want to learn Early African History START HERE*. He also co-authored (with John Matthews) *African Mathematics: History, Textbook and Classroom Lessons*.

In 2015 he wrote *19 Lessons in Black History* and *The Black Musical Tradition and Early Black Literature*. He also wrote *Blacks and Religion Volume Two*.

Speaking Engagements

Looking for a speaker for your next event?

Robin Walker 'The Black History Man' is dynamic and engaging, both as a speaker and a workshop leader. He brings Black or African history alive, making it relevant for the present generation. You will love his perfect blend of accessibility, engagement, and academic rigour where learning becomes fun.

Motivational crowds as well as academic, museum and history society audiences will appreciate his lecture *The Rise and Fall of Black Wall $treet*.

To book Robin Walker for your next event, send an email to historicalwalker@yahoo.com

Flagship Course: *Off The Plantation ... Into Your Own Business*

Would you like to deepen your learning of Black economic empowerment by studying with Robin Walker?

Following in the footsteps of George Subira and believing that poverty is the biggest problem that Black Communities need to solve, 'The Black History Man' has a course on Black economic empowerment which consists of seven content laden seminars:

1. The Challenges faced by the Black Community in Making Money
2. Success and the Power of the Mind
3. An Analysis of the Subira Model of Economic Empowerment

4. Why you Need to be Able to Sell
5. An Analysis of the Empowerment Ideas of *Rich Dad*
6. The Seven Key Empowerment Principles
7. Developing an Action Plan for Individual Empowerment

For more details on this course or any other enquiries, email me at historicalwalker@yahoo.com

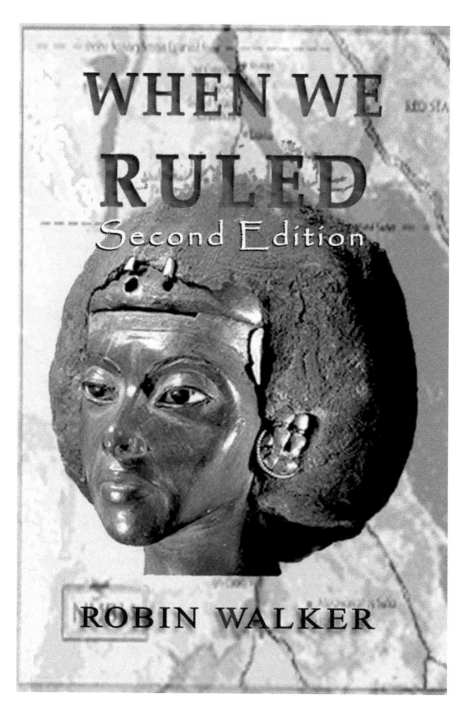

WHEN WE RULED

Second Edition

ROBIN WALKER

Available from www.whenweruled.com

INDEX

Lightning Source UK Ltd.
Milton Keynes UK
UKHW051841101119
353267UK00013B/225/P